What's with St. Louis?

Copyright © 2016 by Reedy Press, LLC
Reedy Press
PO Box 5131
St. Louis, MO 63139, USA
www.reedypress.com

No part of this publication may be reproduced or transmitted in any form or by any means, electronic or mechanical, including photocopy, recording, or any information storage and retrieval system, without permission in writing from the publisher.

Permissions may be sought directly from Reedy Press at the above mailing address or via our website at www.reedypress.com.

Library of Congress Control Number: 2016940395

ISBN: 9781681060507

Design by Jill Halpin

ROLL sign image on cover: Jeff and Randy Vines for STL Style

Printed in the United States of America
16 17 18 19 20   5 4 3 2 1

DEDICATION

For Mike, David, and Ashley.

St. Louis—your hometown.

PREFACE

St. Louie. Mound City. Gateway City. The Lou. River City. STL. Gateway to the West. Whether you're a newcomer or a lifelong resident, St. Louis has much to offer.

Like a colorful patchwork quilt, St. Louis is made up of an assortment of people, locales, foods, activities, and influences that together contribute to its unique character. A mix of old and new, St. Louis looks to the future while keeping an eye on the past. *What's with St. Louis?* provides a glimpse of life in this unique Midwestern city.

St. Louis was established in 1764 along the banks of the Mississippi River near the present-day Gateway Arch grounds. The French who settled there named the village for King Louis IX of France.

Located near the center of the United States, St. Louis became the starting point for those wanting to explore the West, earning it the nickname "Gateway to the West." It also became the stopping point for thousands of immigrants from Europe and other countries who brought with them their dreams of a new life as well as traditions, customs, food, and architectural influences.

St. Louisans embrace diversity, value educational and cultural institutions, and love their sports teams. Think you know everything about St. Louis and those who call it home? Read on!

Valerie Battle Kienzle

CONTENTS

What's with St. Louis?

Valerie Battle Kienzle

REEDY PRESS

What's with the pretzel guys on every corner?

Maybe you've seen them. They hawk paper-wrapped pretzel sticks before sporting events and during rush-hour traffic. The packaging is simple, but one taste will convince you these pretzels are amazing!

St. Louis is one of only three major US cities where vendors sell pretzels on street corners. Gus' Pretzels, a fourth-generation family business and a St. Louis favorite, has supplied pretzels to street vendors for generations. "Street vendors in St. Louis are a solid tradition that hasn't changed for years," says Gus Koebbe III. "Beer and pretzels go hand in hand, and beer and pretzels have been a part of St. Louis for a long time."

"Beer and pretzels go hand in hand"

FOOD

Pretzels were popular in Europe for centuries. The arrival of street-vendor pretzels coincided with the influx of German immigrants to St. Louis in the early twentieth century. The pretzels sold on the street weren't hard and crunchy.

They were soft, chewy sticks of yumminess—and St. Louisans loved them. Since 1920, Gus' has combined the same basic ingredients and no preservatives. "We keep it simple and try to put out the best product possible each day. We make twelve hundred three-ounce pretzel sticks a day and usually sell out."

Who put white Velveeta on my pizza?

Provel—a St. Louis original

"I'll have Provel on that."
Or not.

Unless you're placing a food order in the St. Louis area, this request may be met with a blank stare.

FOOD

Or a follow-up question like, "*You mean provolone?*"

Provel isn't the same as provolone cheese. Provel is a uniquely St. Louis food product obtained by combining three cheeses— processed cheddar, Swiss, and provolone. This combo results in a product that's creamy and less stringy when heated.

Put it on pizza, melt it on a sandwich, or mound it on a salad. However it's served, Provel is a favorite STL taste sensation. The origins of Provel cheese are somewhat a mystery, with several St. Louis families claiming their ancestors created and introduced it in the late 1940s. US Patent and Trademark Office records reveal the product was trademarked in 1950 and that the name "Provel" has no meaning—it's just a jumble of letters.

Provel was popularized locally in the mid-1960s with the introduction of another STL original—Imo's pizza. With its incredibly thin crust, creamy melted Provel, and other toppings, Imo's is crave-worthy. Plus Provel can be ordered and shipped from Imo's.

I'd like a Greek salad, a burek, and a cerveza, please.

STL, home of specialty foods from around the world

One of the great things about an ethnically diverse population is the food. So many recipes for combining ingredients to produce unique, delicious results.

Think of St. Louis as a melting pot of people, customs, and foods. The area's first residents were Native Americans, followed by the French who founded the city of St. Louis in the 1760s. Immigrants from Germany, Italy, Ireland, and Greece flocked here in the 1800s, and African Americans migrated here from the South after the Civil War.

Add to them people from Asia, Bosnia, the Middle East, and Latin America who've settled here in recent years. They've formed communities and brought with them traditional food preparation techniques. The result is a Midwestern city where on any given day a person can sample food from around the world. And that's just for lunch!

 **FOOD**

Try a burek (Bosnian pita bread filled with meat), a cerveza (Spanish for a type of beer), or a St. Paul sandwich (egg foo young patty with mayo, dill pickle, and lettuce on white bread) and prepare to be impressed.

Entrepreneurs have established restaurants throughout the city, like Grbic (Mediterranean cuisine), Pho Grand (Vietnamese), Ranoush (Middle Eastern), and Meskerem (Ethiopian). Others have equipped food trucks to serve an endless array of epicurean delights. As Harry Karagiannis, a founder of the family-run Spiro's Greek Restaurants, says, "Opa!"

Fact BOX

From Rigazzi's signature fish-bowl beers and Tony's award-winning cuisine and ambiance (Missouri's only AAA five-diamond award winner) to Spiro's saganaki (beer-battered, flamed kasseri cheese), St. Louis restaurants offer taste buds a chance to travel the world. And honestly, a night out at one of St. Louis's many delicious ethnic restaurants is considerably cheaper than a round-trip airline ticket!

Brain on rye? With onions?

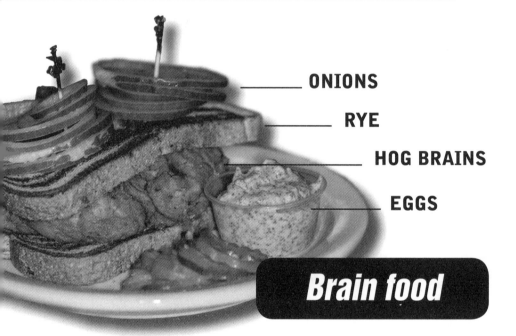

_____ ONIONS

_____ RYE

_____ HOG BRAINS

_____ EGGS

Brain food

BRAINS 25¢ DRIVE IN

🍴 **FOOD**

Ever hear of brain food? St. Louis has had that covered for decades. Does this food make you smarter? No clue. With a consistency like soft-cooked scrambled eggs, it is—quite literally—brains. Hog brains, to be exact.

Schottzie's Bar and Grill's Mike Carlson, thirteen-year veteran and son of co-owner Bob Carlson, says the secret's in the preparation and serving: "We flour and season the brains, shape them into patties, fry them, and serve on rye with hot mustard, dill pickles, and red onions. People love them!"

Brain sandwiches have long been a South St. Louis favorite. Their popularity dates back to the days of the Great Depression when nothing was wasted. Several restaurants offer them, like Fergie's Bar & Restaurant and the Crow's Nest, but Schottzie's reputation spread beyond St. Louis. Andrew Zimmern, host of television's *Bizarre Foods America*, brought his cameras to Schottzie's. "The age of brain sandwich customers is fifty-plus years," Carlson says. "But when that episode airs, we get a lot of younger people who want to try them."

Schottzie's sells fifteen to twenty brain sandwiches each week. The only thing that's changed is the type of brains used. After the Mad Cow Disease scare a few years ago, beef brains were no longer available.

Ravioli can be fried? Who knew?

Toasted ravioli—only in St. Louis

Toasted ravioli

🍴 **FOOD**

Think of tiny pasta squares filled with a dab of ground meat, spinach, and spices. Coat the squares with bread crumbs and fry to a golden brown. That's toasted ravioli, and once you try one, you'll want more—lots more.

As with other St. Louis originals (think gooey butter cake), toasted ravioli began as a mistake. Italian immigrants came to St. Louis more than a century ago and settled in a section of South St. Louis dubbed the Hill. They brought a strong work ethic and generations-old family recipes. Some opened restaurants.

The story goes that in the 1940s a chef accidentally dropped a few ravioli into hot oil instead of boiling water. Curiosity motivated the sampling of the fried, crunchy mistake, and they were declared delicious! Served with marinara sauce and parmesan cheese, these small tasty pillows soon appeared on menus as "toasted" ravioli, and people loved them.

Several local restaurants claim to be the originators of toasted ravioli. "T-ravs are a St. Louis staple and we use the original recipe," says Charlie Gitto's Restaurant employee Samantha Vogt. Owner Charlie Gitto has been featured on the Travel Channel detailing the time-consuming, multistep process his employees use to make the ravioli. And in case you're wondering, the restaurant sells about ten thousand ravioli each week. They're just that good!

Pork Steaks
sound fancy, butt . . .

It's tough being the butt of jokes, but when something's this tasty, maybe that's not such a bad thing.

Stop by any St. Louis grocery store and look for pork steaks. You can't miss them. They're cheap, usually packaged to serve a crowd, and with lots of marbling—definitely not heart-healthy.

But visit a grocery store outside the STL area and you probably won't find them. Ask a butcher where the pork steaks are located and he or she will probably give you that blank look meaning, "I have no idea what you're talking about."

FOOD

In reality, pork steaks aren't steaks at all. They're cut from the part of the pork shoulder often referred to as the Boston butt. But do give this economical local favorite a try. Slap those fat-marbled meat chunks on a hot grill, add a little seasoning, and listen to them sizzle. Cook, flipping occasionally until seared and no pink remains. If you're a fan of sauced pork, add another local favorite, Maull's Barbeque Sauce. Nothing says summer in St. Louis like pork steaks!

Pork Steaks

Another wedding,
another plate of mostaccioli

FOOD

14

It's been showing up at St. Louis wedding receptions for years. Not the cake or fruit punch. Not the creamy mints or nuts.

We're talking about mostaccioli—the dish made with a bit of ground beef, seasoned spaghetti sauce, and tube-shaped, Italian-inspired mostaccioli noodles. Highly economical, filling, and great for feeding crowds of distant relatives who show up for buffet dinners.

St. Louis has a sizable population of Italian descent, but this pasta dish isn't just served at Italian receptions. St. Louisans of all ethnicities enjoy a healthy serving or two of the stuff, often topped with a sprinkling of Parmesan cheese.

But if you want to taste really *good* mostaccioli, head to a restaurant like Zia's on the Hill and order the baked mostaccioli. Made with a hearty marinara sauce, melted Italian cheese, and parmigiana, it's truly a taste of Italy.

The Slinger

St. Louis was home to legendary cookbook author Irma Rombauer (*The Joy of Cooking*), but her famous volume doesn't contain a recipe for the slinger.

Think late nights and early mornings, the craving for something greasy. Think about a combination of diner foods layered on one plate—eggs, hash browns, meat patty, chili. And don't forget cheese, onions, jalapenos, and hot sauce on the side.

That's the slinger—a St. Louis original.

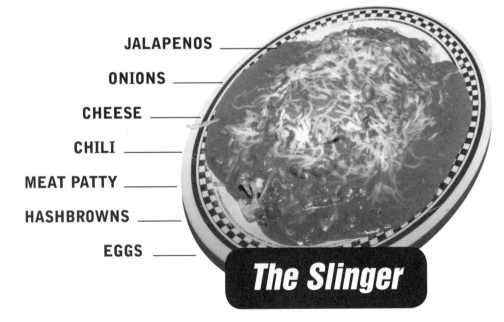

JALAPENOS

ONIONS

CHEESE

CHILI

MEAT PATTY

HASHBROWNS

EGGS

The Slinger

FOOD

You really gonna eat that?

"There's always been lots of hearsay about how the slinger came about," says Marji Rugg, daughter of Courtesy Diner owner Larry Rugg. "Dad says it's just always been around." Whatever its origin, generations of St. Louisans have feasted on this flavor amalgamation.

Some may wonder how anything with so many components can taste good, but those who eat them swear to the tasty appeal. "On weekends during third shift, we serve about sixty slingers each night," Rugg says. "During first shift, it can go as high as 150. And calorie count for a slinger is 1,300–1,500 calories!" Don't plan on eating again for a while.

Donut obsessed, perhaps?

St. Louisans love that fried dough!

The next time you crave a donut, give your mouth something to savor. St. Louis has several dozen locally owned and operated donut shops.

FOOD

Terry Clanton, owner of World's Fair Donuts near the Missouri Botanical Garden, starts his work day at 4:30 a.m. He's been making donuts every day for the last forty years. Like his father before him, he takes pride in keeping his loyal customers supplied in donuts.

"We make traditional donuts like cake, jelly, custard, and long johns," Clanton says. "We don't try to introduce new or unusual ingredient combos. We stick with what we do best and what our customers enjoy."

Some locals enjoy visiting small shops like Clanton's where the donuts are lined up like soldiers. Others call ahead with orders and pick them up at drive-through windows. Regardless of where they're purchased, it's difficult to find a bad donut in St. Louis. Low-calorie they're not, nor are they Paleo diet–compatible.

And if you're one of those people who need to justify the consumption of multiple donuts, check out the mini-donuts at the Soulard Farmers Market. Smaller donuts have fewer calories, so you can eat more than one, right? And what's not to love about a good local sugar high?

How can cake be *gooey?*

Gooey Butter Cake

 **FOOD**

It's one of those foods with a somewhat questionable background. Some say it was a mixing mistake. Others blame the order of ingredients. Regardless, it's a St. Louis tradition dating back to the early twentieth

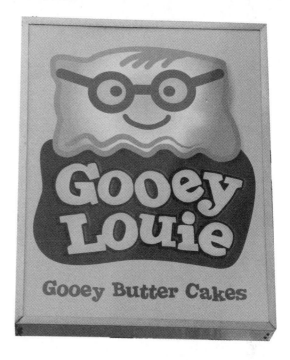

century that's loaded with calories, but oh so delicious.

Gooey butter cake is often described as not really cake, custard, pie, or Danish, but a sweet confection that has elements of all of the above.

"It's a very traditional St. Louis item," says Talan Cooksey of Park Avenue Coffee, a Lafayette Square eatery specializing in gooey butter cake. "We have seventy-three official flavors, but traditional, triple chocolate, and white chocolate raspberry are our most popular flavors. We usually have eight or nine flavors available on any given day."

Park Avenue Coffee's gooey butter cakes are so popular they're carried in twenty St. Louis locations, including retail outlets and farmers markets. They've been featured on the *Today* show and the Food Network. Plus they're shipped throughout the world. "Gooey butter cakes are uniquely St. Louis," says Cooksey.

Meat processing done the old-fashioned way

G & W Bavarian Style Sausage Company

FOOD

St. Louis's German heritage roots run deep. Few places is this more obvious than the Wanninger family's G & W Bavarian Style Sausage Company, where the company slogan is, "You can't beat G & W Meat!"

"This is a third-generation family business, with the fourth generation coming on," says Mel Wanninger. "The recipes we use were brought to the United States from the family butcher shop in Germany."

The company's twenty employees process three to five thousand pounds of meat each week, everything from specialty sausages like andouille, bockworst, chorizo, Polish hot links, Bavarian-style Landjager beef stick, and Cajun chicken sausage to deer meat. The company's products are sold at Dierbergs supermarkets, C-Rallo Meat Market in O'Fallon, Dunn's Sporting Goods, and some area convenience stores.

"We shut down our regular meat processing in the fall and do nothing but process deer meat for two or three weeks," says Wanninger. The company also participates in the Share the Harvest program, where deer hunters drop off deer, the company processes it, and the meat is given to food banks and homeless shelters.

Why did the chicken cross the road?

Hodak's Restaurant & Bar

If you're cruising through South St. Louis and looking for a place to eat, stop by Hodak's Restaurant & Bar and order the fried chicken. FYI, this isn't your basic chain-restaurant fried chicken. Prepare to be impressed! Hodak's chicken is so good your taste buds will soon be crowing.

The Hodak's people have been doing what they do best since 1962. And the eighty-five employees must be doing something right. Manager Jose Batres says the restaurant goes through ten thousand pounds of chicken each week. That's a lot of poultry!

FOOD

Breaded fried chicken is the restaurant's specialty and biggest seller. "We sell a lot of half chickens, but also have four varieties of chicken wings," Batres says. The fried chicken has been voted St. Louis's best for the last twenty-five years. The restaurant serves lunch and dinner, caters, provides takeouts, and has a banquet room. Its reputation speaks for itself.

Why do I feel like I'm in an outdoor sauna?

The Lou's high humidity

Clothing feels **damp**

Skin feels **sticky**

Mouth is **dry**

Hair is **frizzy**

TEMPERATURE AND HUMIDITY.	7 A. M.	10·20 A. M.	2 P. M.	2·30 P. M.	9 P. M.	
January 1, 1881:						
Thermometer, degrees Fahr.....	4	12	27·5	29·5	30	
Relative humidity, per cent.....	74	61	76	73	68	
Actual humidity, grains........	0·44	0·59	1·35	1·35	1·35	
June 1, 1881:						
Thermometer, degrees Fahr.....	73	78	79	80	70	6
Relative humidity, per cent.....	72	61	54	51	80	85
Actual humidity, grains........	6·36	6·46	5·95	5·76	6·41	6

Ah, summer in St. Louis. What is it about this land-locked part of the US that makes summertime so humid and uncomfortable?

"The Gulf of Mexico is the St. Louis region's primary source of humidity and heat in some part as well," says Jon Carney, meteorologist with the National Weather Service in St. Louis. "There's not much between us and the Gulf except for the Ozarks, and if we didn't have the Gulf, the Great Plains and Mississippi Valley would be a desert. The warmest days occur when there is a very large ridge of high pressure aloft accompanied by west or southwest wind blowing downslope from the Great Plains or Ozark Plateau. As air descends, it compresses and heats up.

"Also, agriculture in the region can add humidity locally through evapotranspiration."

But it's difficult to be happy when you walk outside and instantly break into a drenching sweat. Is St. Louis weather unusual? "Actually, no," says Carney. "Our weather is pretty typical for cities at our latitude and elevation above sea level."

Is an earthquake really possible?

New Madrid, the San Andreas of the Midwest

Shake, rattle, and roll. Anyone who's experienced a small earthquake or tremor can attest to a feeling of helplessness as the ground and everything attached to it moves.

Shortly after 2 a.m. on December 16, 1811, residents of tiny New Madrid, Missouri, felt the first tremor of a series of earthquakes. The earth opened with large fissures, the nearby Mississippi River generated tremendous waves, and thousands of trees, islands, and buildings were destroyed. A second, stronger earthquake occurred January 23, 1812, followed by a third on February 7, 1812. The quakes caused damage hundreds of miles away, including St. Louis. They were deemed the worst in US history.

Since then, people living in southeastern Missouri have feared another severe earthquake. Infrequent small tremors serve as reminders of what could happen. Is an earthquake along the New Madrid fault a serious possibility?

WEATHER

"Yes, there are small earthquakes on the New Madrid fault all the time, usually several every month," says Jon Carney, meteorologist with the National Weather Service in St. Louis. "They're small and we don't feel them way up here. If New Madrid ever cut loose with a really big earthquake, it would be a disaster."

NEW MADRID

(Continued from other side)

The New Madrid Earthquake, made up of a series of monstrous and lesser shocks, which began Dec. 16, 1811, and continued over a year, centered here. One of the great earthquakes of the world because of severity and length it caused little loss of life in a thinly settled region. Some of the shocks were felt as far as 1100 miles. Reelfoot Lake across the river is a result of the disaster. New Madrid land certificates, good for public land elsewhere, were provided sufferers by U.S. relief act, 1815, which benefited mostly speculators.

In 1862 Union forces captured New Madrid and by means of a "canal" sawed through a submerged forest to a bayou, gained control of Island No. 10 and command of the river. Nearby in Mississippi Co. is Belmont battlefield, scene of an 1861 engagement in which both Federal forces under Grant and Confederates under Pillow claimed victory.

New Madrid, seat of government of one of 5 Spanish districts, later one of Missouri's first 5 counties, serves a farming community. Cotton and soybean crops predominate. Rich land has been reclaimed by the Little River and St. Johns Levee drainage systems.

Erected by State Historical Society of Missouri and State Highway Commission, 1953

Auntie Em, why is everyone running to the basement?

St. Louis—a severe weather magnet

People talk about St. Louis weather extremes. Temperatures can reach the seventies in January, and then it snows in April. Why such variations?

"From a forecaster's perspective, the weather here is unique because we sit in a region where we experience all four seasons," says meteorologist Jon Carney of the National Weather Service in St. Louis. "We have extremes primarily because of geography. There's not much between us and the Gulf of Mexico, and there's nothing between us and the Arctic except a few wire fences. Cold air masses can rush south with no geographical impediment, and warm air masses can rush north and east with very little geographical impediment. However, we're actually no more susceptible to severe weather than any other Midwestern/Great Plains city.

WEATHER

"We do have some bad floods though, and that's because about one quarter of the continental US drains right past St. Louis on the Missouri and Mississippi Rivers," Carney continues. "That's a lot of water. Mostly St. Louis weather is mild but with a few days of extreme weather each year, which makes forecasting challenging. This is a great place to study the profession of meteorology."

Fact BOX

If the weather in St. Louis seems wetter and warmer than you remember in years past, it is. "Beginning in the early 1980s, an unprecedented wet period has evolved in Missouri," says Pat Guinan, University of Missouri Extension state climatologist.

"Over the past few decades, all four seasons have witnessed more above-normal precipitation years in Missouri, most notable in winter and spring. Missouri's most recent warm annual temperature trend began in the mid-1980s, and 2012 was the warmest year on record since 1895," Guinan continues. "Seasonally, Missouri winters and springs have experienced the greatest warming trend and snowfall trends have been declining."

"Some of this warming effect is likely due to urbanization, and some of it is likely due to broad-scale climate change," says meteorologist Jon Carney of the National Weather Service in St. Louis.

This so-called "river" is everywhere, but where's the water?

The River des Peres, STL's man-made waterway

Cruise the streets of southwestern St. Louis and you'll see it. Just over there is the River des Peres. Signs, paved basin, bridges, protective fencing. It's all there—but often no water. No cascading ripples. Not even a trickle. So why all the infrastructure for something that isn't?

To truly understand the River des Peres (French for River of the Fathers), a small stream noted as early as the 1700s, it's necessary to travel back in St. Louis history. Step back to the days of cesspools, standing rainwater, and flooded low-lying ground. In other words, to the days before the establishment of an underground sewer system for rainwater and other liquid wastes. STL was smelly and unsanitary.

Wanting to impress visitors to the Louisiana Purchase Exposition (1904 World's Fair), politicians made decisions that would have a lasting impact on St. Louis. Channels were dug, water rerouted underground, and natural streams diverted to connect to what became an eighteen-mile-long channel and the backbone of St. Louis's sewer system.

 **WATER**

The River des Peres seldom fills its designated path. In the summer, the outdoor sections become home to greenery, frogs, and turtles. The underground sections provide shelter for snakes and rats. But when the spring rains fall for days on end, the river-that-isn't can become raging floodwaters filled with fish from outlying tributaries. And only rarely (the flood of 1993) does the river overflow its man-made banks and flood surrounding areas. Most days the river is an ecological playground in an expansive concrete trench.

The Mississippi River looks pretty brown and determined—like those big birds over there.

Bald eagles and other migratory birds spend their winters in St. Louis.

Welcome to St. Louis—home of the Gateway Arch, the Cardinals, and migratory birds.

St. Louis sits near the confluence of three major waterways—the Mississippi, Missouri, and Illinois Rivers. Generations of humans found the location ideal for transportation and trade. Generations of migratory birds including eagles, Canada geese, ducks, snow geese, and swans found that it's a great place to spend the winter.

 **WATER**

"We're right on the Mississippi flyway," says Pat Behle of the Columbia Bottom Conservation Area, part of the Missouri Department of Conservation. "It's typical for migratory birds to follow the Mississippi north to south and south to north. They're looking for a place to eat and a place to rest. Water and vegetation, wetlands. We have them."

Water near the rivers' dams is constantly churning. The surface doesn't freeze, making an assortment of fish readily available for hungry birds. Tall trees and bluffs near the rivers provide ideal lookout and roosting locations.

Most of the area's eagle sightings happen during January and February, but a few eagles remain year-round, says Behle. "What makes St. Louis unique is that we have the confluence of these great rivers. It's the third or fourth largest watershed in the world, and these birds have been doing this forever."

Waterworks Standpipes

Early water towers combined form and function.

Drive through the city of St. Louis and you'll probably see them. They're tall, thin, artistically crafted, and look totally out of place in today's world. Only seven of the hundreds built in the US more than a hundred years ago remain. St. Louis is home to three of them, and they're listed on the National Register of Historic Places.

It was the end of the nineteenth century, and St. Louis was one of the largest US cities. As the population grew, so too did the demand for water. At that time, steam pumps sent water through residential and commercial buildings' pipes, but they weren't dependable for getting water to upper floors. To help control pressure surges in water pipes, large cities built vertical standpipes. Water rose and fell inside the standpipes and helped prevent surges. Decorative towers were built to conceal the pipes.

St. Louis's first standpipe water tower was built in 1871 on Grand Avenue. The Grand "Old White" tower is topped with decorative iron leaf work and remained in service until 1912. The Bissell "New Red" tower was built between 1885 and 1886 from red brick with terra cotta and gray stone accents. It remained in use until 1912. The Compton Hill tower is the youngest of STL's standpipes. Built in 1898, it was used until 1929. Through the years various factions supported tearing down the standpipes, but preservationists were successful in keeping the architectural relics intact.

More breweries than you can shake a stein at

St. Louisans love their beer!

A toast to the nineteenth-century German immigrants who made St. Louis a leader in malt beverage production—and consumption. If not for their unhappiness in das vaterland, thousands of Germans might have stayed put. Instead, they heard about an idyllic place called Missouri, USA, and flocked here.

DRINK UP

They came to St. Louis in search of a new life. They arrived with few possessions, a strong work ethic, and family recipes for beer.

Breweries popped up all over town. St. Louisans quenched their thirsts with home-town brews like Budweiser, Falstaff, Griesedieck, Lemp's, ABC Bohemian, Hyde Park, Gast, and Schorr-Kolkschneider. Some lasted a short time. Others remain top-sellers today. What was true then is true today—we love beer!

And our taste for all things beer hasn't diminished. St. Louis is home to microbreweries, brewpubs, and regional craft breweries, including Urban Chestnut Brewing Company and Saint Louis Brewery with Schlafly products.

With two consumption venues, forty to fifty different beer offerings each year, a growing Midwestern market, and plans for in-house taste-test and research capabilities, Urban Chestnut is blazing new paths in the craft brewing segment. According to co-owner and brewmeister Florian Kuplent, "We are unique. We have two unique locations and two beer series, Revolution and Reverence, plus we're always developing new beers."

Urban Chestnut has more than one hundred employees and a nontraditional business plan. "We have no PR people; we do everything in-house," Kuplent says. "We're committed to sustainability (the Manchester Avenue location is LEED certified). We recycle 95 percent of the waste produced, conserve water, and plan to set up a city garden to grow products for our beers and restaurants."

Built on the foundations of the past, with an eye to the future, today's St. Louis brewing industry thrives!

Beer
was once stored underground?

**Talk about a man cave.
Natural refrigeration, St. Louis style.**

St. Louis became home to thousands of German immigrants in the 1800s. Many arrived here with brewing recipes from the Old Country and a love of beer. How convenient to discover the cool, dark confines of a series of caves spread beneath their newly adopted city. Natural bier storage facilities!

The location of some breweries was determined by their proximity to the underground caves. Industrious brewers reinforced the caves with stone and wooden timbers and built tunnels.

Then the twentieth century arrived and eventually artificial refrigeration. The caves were no longer needed. Time passed and most of the caves' entrances were lost or blocked due to above-ground development.

Do the caves still exist? "Yes, they do," says Andrew Weil of the

DRINK UP

Landmarks Association of St. Louis. Some are said to be located beneath South St. Louis's Benton Park area and structures that once housed the Lemp Brewery.

But don't make plans to turn those ancient underground compartments into modern man caves. "Some are accessible," says Weil. But have they been structurally reinforced? "Not to my knowledge."

Fact BOX

Missouri is nicknamed "the Cave State." According to the Missouri Department of Natural Resources, the state has more than fifty-six hundred recorded caves. Some, like Meramec Caverns and Onondaga Cave, are called show caves and are open to the public. Others, called wild caves, are located on private property. In 1980, the Missouri legislature passed the Cave Resources Act to protect the state's caves from vandalism and wild caves from trespassers. Those who enjoy exploring caves are called "spelunkers" or simply "cavers."

The ghosts of soft drinks past

St. Louis, an incubator for soft drink development

Necessity is the mother of invention, or so an old saying goes. St. Louis is famous for beer. Generations downed our brews. That is, until the unfortunate inconvenience known as Prohibition. From 1920 to 1933, US companies ceased malt beverage production.

Suddenly multitudes of people were without work. How would the local laborers who made glass bottles and wooden pallets, who handled raw materials and produced and distributed beer, support themselves and their families?

The answer was soft drinks.

Ingenious industry leaders repurposed materials and equipment to manufacture nonalcoholic, malt-free beverages. And workers were back on the job. Products like Howdy Orange, 7UP, Orange Smile, Whistle, Vess, and IBC Root Beer, were born in St. Louis.

"The manufacture of soft drinks got people back to work," says Greg R. Rhomberg, lifelong St. Louis memorabilia collector, amateur local history buff, and owner of Antique Warehouse. "Besides, people needed something to mix with their illegally produced home brews and moonshine!"

Traces of St. Louis's soft drink past remain visible. The Orange Smile Sirup Company building, located at Ninth and Soulard, has been repurposed for residential living. A

🍷 **DRINK UP**

somewhat faded twelve-foot Vess soda bottle stands near I-70 in downtown St. Louis. With its mid-twentieth-century graphics, it's a reminder of St. Louis's soft drink history.

And for the last twenty-plus years, Fitz's soft drinks have called STL home. Fitz's may not have a global presence, but a taste of the company's locally produced flagship root beer or cream, orange, or cherry soda is a throwback to a different era. The drinks are crisp, flavorful, and sweetened with natural cane sugar. No high fructose corn syrup here!

Fitz's Root Beer began here in the 1940s but faded into obscurity. In 1993, tiny Fitz's Bottling Company opened in the Delmar Loop, featuring a vintage 1940s bottling machine and original product formulas. Then, as now, customers at the adjoining restaurant watch with fascination as a line of clean glass bottles snakes its way from empty to filled, capped, and ready for consumption. Bigger isn't necessarily better!

Fact BOX

C. L. Grigg was an entrepreneur. He also knew how to keep a secret. Although many speculated about the origin of the name he gave his Depression-era lemon-lime soft drink, he never revealed it. The most frequent guess? The sparkling product got its name because it contained seven ingredients. Guess we'll never know for sure why the UNcola was called 7UP!

The flavor extract for 7UP is derived from oils taken from the outer peelings of fresh lemons and limes. The fruits' pulp, juice, and seeds are waste products.

Anyone from here sleeping with the fishes?

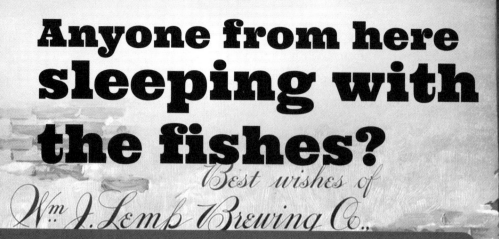

Best wishes of

W.ⁿ J. Lemp Brewing Co.,

STL's organized crime connection

Once upon a time, St. Louis had connections to organized crime, specifically the Mafia.

Blame it on implementation in 1920 of the Eighteenth Amendment to the US Constitution, prohibiting the manufacture, distribution, and sale of alcoholic beverages. Such restrictions in a city that loves its beer and spirits was bound to cause an uproar.

It's the principle of supply and demand. It wasn't long before enterprising underground networks took advantage of the opportunity to supply the demands of thirsty St. Louisans. Complex syndicates functioned here as well as in other major cities, including Chicago, Detroit, and, Cleveland.

"The Mafia had connections in St. Louis, but they are diminished now," says Robert Lowery Sr., a member of St. Louis's Major Case Squad, the St. Louis Strike Force on Organized Crime, and a former city of Florissant mayor. Lowery attributes the decline in the Mafia's St. Louis presence to successful law enforcement and younger generations not wanting to become involved.

VIEWS OF ST. LOUIS, MO.

Hoosier? But I'm not from Indiana.

The peculiar vocabulary of St. Louisans

Many places in the US have them. They're words that by their mere utterance conjure images of a stereotype—and not necessarily a positive one.

In St. Louis, the word "hoosier" has nothing to do with the state of Indiana or your grandmother's antique kitchen cabinet. To label someone a hoosier means the person can be classified based on certain stereotypical parameters.

For example, a St. Louis hoosier leaves the Christmas tree in the family room year-round, merely covering it with a sheet when it's not the holiday season. A St. Louis hoosier keeps plastic flowers in outdoor pots—even when the temperature is -10°. Why? Because they look pretty and add a pop of color. Never mind that they're weighted down by six inches of snow! A St. Louis hoosier shops at the grocery store with a head full of pink plastic hair rollers, but covers them with a colorful scarf and dons lipstick because she might run into someone she knows.

You get the idea.

Uniquely St. Louis pronunciations

Blame it on the French settlers of the 1760s. Or blame it on later immigrants who learned English as a second language.

Call it vernacular or folk vocabulary, St. Louis has unique word pronunciations. They start as mispronunciations and eventually become part of local speech. "Every major population center features regional and ethnic variants in pronunciation, grammar, or word choice," says University of Missouri–St. Louis's Dr. Benjamin Torbert. "St. Louis's combination of variants generally owes to its geography and history, different ethnic and linguistic inputs.

"St. Louis's language reflects its people, so we boast an array of influence," he continues. "This is a natural process—when speakers borrow a word from another language, they change it to fit their own language, somewhat."

In St. Louis, roof sounds like "ruff," wash and washed are pronounced "warsh" and "warsht," across is "acrost," "Dezember" sounds German, sandwich becomes "sammich," and a twenty-five-cent coin is pronounced "quater." Interstate 44 is pronounced "Farty-Far" and an ice cream sundae is pronounced "sunduh."

"I would say that most large US cities have their own unique word pronunciations," says Washington University's Dr. Brett Hyde. "If they are large enough, they might have several distinct varieties."

St. Louis Post-Dispatch columnist Joe Holleman agrees. "New York does. Chicago does. They're neither right nor wrong. They're just uniquely that city, a different way of saying things.

"What's different about St. Louisans is that they apologize for their mispronunciations. New Yorkers don't apologize for anything!"

The Fourth City?
What were the first three?

St. Louis, one of America's top cities

 WHAT'S IN A WORD?

Newspaperman Logan Uriah Reavis had big dreams following the Civil War. He wanted to make St. Louis one of the country's premier cities. He campaigned to have the nation's capital, including its buildings, relocated from Washington, D.C., to St. Louis. A national conference was held here and plans were discussed. Obviously the move never happened.

The 1860 US census showed St. Louis with a larger population than Chicago. But in 1856 Chicago opened the Chicago

```
Rank Place                          Population
---------------------------------------------
  1  New York city, NY ........  3,437,202
  2  Chicago city, IL..........  1,698,575
  3  Philadelphia city, PA.....  1,293,697
  4  St. Louis city, MO........    575,238
```

and Rock Island Railroad bridge across the Mississippi River, a move important to the city's commercial transportation and growth. St. Louis's Eads Bridge didn't open across the Mississippi until 1874. St. Louis leaders worried that the 1870 census would put Chicago's population ahead of St. Louis's. Not ones to let the truth stand in the way
of a good story, they inflated the census figures.

But the 1880 census figures didn't lie. Chicago had the larger population.

Population growth in St. Louis continued. By 1900, St. Louis was indeed ranked the nation's fourth-largest city. And in 1904, the world came to St. Louis for the Louisiana Purchase Exhibition, a world's fair like no other.

How did I pass through eight cities in three miles driving down one road?

St. Louis and the abundance of small municipalities

CITY LIMIT
Sycamore Hills
POP 668

STREET TALK

The city of St. Louis has some seventy-nine neighborhood areas, including private streets, historically renovated residences, and working-class and industrial sections. These include the Central West End, Soulard, Benton Park, Bevo Mill, Carondelet, Baden, the Hill, Penrose, O'Fallon, and Tower Grove East.

In 2015, St. Louis County contained ninety municipalities, some of which are small and many of which have their own municipal services. These include Maplewood, Marlborough, Brentwood, Grantwood Village, Crestwood, and University City. Roads like Olive, Gravois, and Delmar run for miles, taking drivers from parts of the city of St. Louis and on through St. Louis County municipalities. Bound on the east by the Mississippi River, St. Louis grew and expanded north, south, and west from its original village settlement along the river.

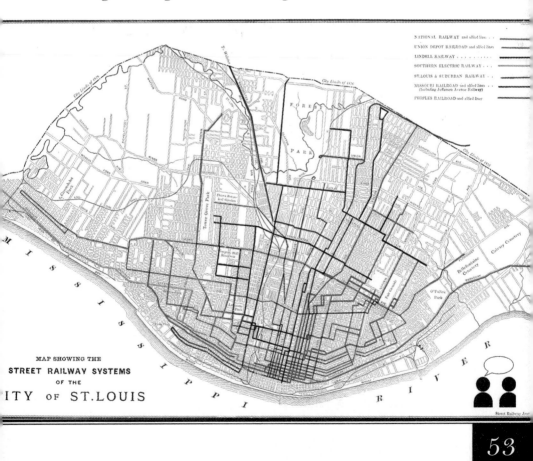

The rolling stop:
a St. Louis tradition

According to the St. Louis Department of Streets, the city has approximately one thousand miles of streets (not including hundreds of alleys). And if you ask drivers who live in or commute to the city, it contains about a million stop signs. At least it seems that way.

"In reality, the city has twenty-two thousand stop signs,"

says Stephen J. Runde, director of streets. Contrary to what some drivers may think, stop signs aren't randomly placed at locations as an inconvenience. Stop signs, as well as all traffic control devices, have a purpose. Their purpose is to enhance traffic flow and improve safety for drivers as well as pedestrians.

STREET TALK

St. Louis, like some other large metropolises, has a dense street grid. Major arterial roadways run through the city, intersected by hundreds of secondary and cross streets. Factors such as traffic and pedestrian volume, speed, high accident rates, and limited visibility are considered prior to stop sign installation.

However, some areas seem to have an excessive number of stop signs. Drivers can hardly accelerate before needing to brake again for another stop sign. Therefore, quick glances and reduced acceleration (but not complete stops) have become commonplace on St. Louis streets—a.k.a. the rolling stop.

As defined by the St. Louis, Missouri, Code of Ordinances, ordinance 17.02.500, "'Stop' means the complete cessation from movement." Failure to do so can result in citations and fines. Something to keep in mind the next time you roll through a stop sign.

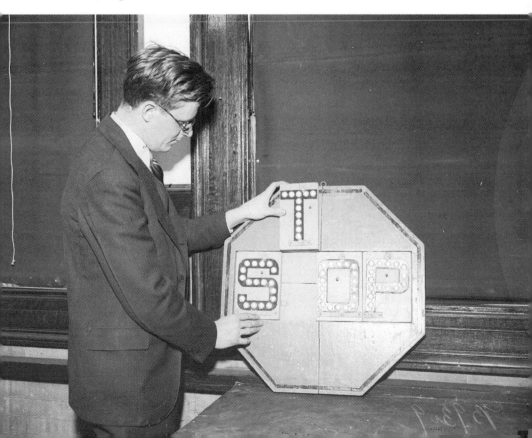

Can you still get your kicks on Route 66?

The Mother Road is still alive in St. Louis.

US Route 66 has been the inspiration for songs, movies, and a television show. It was built at a time when automobiles enabled Americans to become a more mobile society. It connected Chicago, Illinois, to Santa Monica, California, and it didn't take long for it to become known as America's Main Street.

Route 66 traversed through small towns in eight states. Missouri was one of those states. Soon filling (gas) stations, diners, motor courts, merchants, and tourist sights popped up along the route.

Route 66 in Missouri began in the late 1920s. It was formed by piecing together decades-old trade and stage coach trails. It went up and down hills, around curves and beside scenic views. It came through the city of St. Louis and included parts of existing city streets (Grand,

 STREET TALK

Delmar, Lindell, Boyle). It has been realigned numerous times through the years.

Although US Route 66 has been decommissioned, original sections of it remain in the St. Louis area. St. Louis lawyer Norma M. Bolin conducted extensive research into the history of Route 66 after watching the movie *Cars*. The movie piqued her interest in the Mother Road. "The road continued to evolve in St. Louis, and some of the decades-old original structures still exist," she says. "I've read up on it and fell in love with the mom-and-pop operations along it. I decided if I didn't get this information down, it was going to be lost."

Seattle, Washington, claims to have been the location for the first gas station in 1907. However, St. Louis was the location of the first filling station in 1905. The St. Louis station offered drive-through refueling services for the increasingly popular automobile.

The first paving in Missouri happened in 1932 along part of St. Louis's Watson Road. Soon that section of roadway was incorporated into US Route 66.

Cherokee Street
(more than a people, more than a tribe)

FURNITURE

A popular STL street and neighborhood

French settlers established a village here in the 1760s and called it St. Louis. A grid pattern was established with streets named for trees and US presidents, and in South St. Louis some were named for Native American tribes and rivers.

One such thoroughfare was Cherokee Street. With the arrival of electric streetcar lines in the 1890s, Cherokee Street became a residential and commercial hub. Dry goods and furniture stores, tailors, doctors, butchers, and milliners were there, as well as photography studios, barbershops, and saloons. No need to travel downtown.

The demise of streetcars and the popularity of automobiles and suburban shopping centers took a toll on Cherokee Street in the last half of the twentieth century, but today it is again a thriving destination. "Four dense, diverse neighborhoods surround Cherokee Street and are filled with passionate people engaged in their communities," says Cherokee Street liaison Anne McCullough. "Community here means business owners, artists, residents, and property owners invested in each other, committed to supporting inclusivity and diversity.

"Cherokee Street really has everything one might need—groceries, furniture, coffee, live music, art, pet shops, galleries, salons, barbershops, beer, office space, clothing, flowers, and plants."

Fact BOX

South St. Louis streets named for Native American tribes and rivers include Potomac, Winnebago, Keokuk, Miami, Osage, Pontiac, Gasconade, Shenandoah, Powhatan, Hiawatha, Susquehanna, and Osceola.

Why are St. Louis's downtown streets named for trees?

An arborist's delight

It was 1764. Pierre Laclede, his lieutenant Auguste Chouteau, and thirty men settled on the banks of the Mississippi River and began to build a trading village. The tiny settlement had three north-south streets and three east-west streets. Being of French descent, the settlers naturally gave the streets French names: The north-south streets were named La Grande Rue, Rue d'Eglise, and Rue des Granges. The east-west streets were named La Rue de la Tour, Rue de la Place, and Rue Missouri.

The streets were still known by their French names until 1809. From that time until 1826, the east-west streets were known by letters of the alphabet, along with a North or South prefix. In 1826, the city of St. Louis adopted the street-naming system originated by the city of Philadelphia. North-south streets were given number names (First, Second). East-west streets were named for trees (Chestnut, Walnut).

Fact BOX

Time passed. The names of some of the tree streets were changed to honor individuals important during St. Louis's early years. Hazel became Chouteau, Cherry became Franklin, Mulberry became Gratiot, Willow became Biddle, Plum became Cerre, and Myrtle became Clark.

PINE ST

Riding the Rails

Railroading in St. Louis

St. Louis was a commerce center long before railroads. Its proximity to the Mississippi, Missouri, and Illinois Rivers, plus its location near the center of the country, made it an ideal transportation crossroads.

Railroads in Missouri were discussed as early as 1836, but construction of iron railroads didn't begin in St. Louis until 1851. Plans included small operations and multiple connector routes. The Eads Bridge, completed in 1874 and the first to span the Mississippi River, changed railroading in St. Louis. It and other railroad bridges made St. Louis a focal point of cross-continent commerce. Previously, freight was unloaded from trains onto ferries to cross the rivers and then reloaded onto trains.

In 1889, multiple railroads joined together to form the Terminal Railroad Association of St. Louis (TRRA). "TRRA was formed to construct and control railroad facilities and operations for the benefit of the owning railroads," says Ronald N. Zimmer, a fifty-year veteran of railway and waterways engineering and Museum of Transportation volunteer. "The role of the TRRA has been to transfer railcars from one railroad's yard to another's, providing interchange services. TRRA exists today."

STREET TALK

The TRRA was also responsible for building Union Station, which opened in 1894. "Union Station provided for all passenger activity at a single location since St. Louis was a termination point for all railroads," says Zimmer. "If your destination was not St. Louis, you could transfer from one train to another without moving to another station. Compare this with Chicago, which had at least five railroad stations, each serving a different group of railroads."

By the 1940s, approximately one hundred thousand passengers a day passed through Union Station on their way to or from a train. Union Station was designated a national historic landmark in 1976 and was restored in 1985.

Fact BOX

"Railroads may be as strong today as at any time in the past, both here and throughout the nation, but the nature of their business has changed," says Ronald N. Zimmer. "Almost all trackage in the St. Louis area is in fairly intensive use. However, the manner of use has changed. Door-to-door rail service for manufactured items is rarely economical today and lacks flexibility. This system has been replaced by containers (trailer bodies of typical highway trucks) that are loaded at factories, driven to rail yards, loaded on trains for long-distance trips, and then driven to their final destination. Containers hold a wide variety of manufactured goods such as electronics and garments. Trains in the St. Louis area also carry a lot of coal and sometimes windmill generator components, including 150-foot-long blades." Railroads operating in the St. Louis area today include the Union Pacific, BNSF, CSX, Norfolk Southern, Kansas City Southern, TRRA, and Amtrak. Several small railroads serve specific industrial areas.

I'm on Lindbergh Blvd., wait North Kirkwood Road, wait Lindbergh? And why isn't one Watson enough?

What's in a street name? Apparently a lot. And in St. Louis, names change.

It was a big deal when James P. Kirkwood brought the Pacific Railroad to St. Louis in 1850. Now people could live in outlying areas and commute to work in St. Louis.

Suburban St. Louis living was born in 1853 with the founding of Kirkwood, the first planned residential community west of the Mississippi River. It was common at that time to name streets for US presidents. "Except Kirkwood residents didn't like Presidents Tyler and Polk," says Sue Burkett, Kirkwood Historical Society librarian. "They decided to name Kirkwood's main thoroughfare for American statesman Daniel Webster."

Webster Avenue existed in Kirkwood for more than sixty years. It was called Denny Road north and south of Kirkwood's city limits.

STREET TALK

Then people complained that Webster Avenue and Webster Groves, a nearby suburb, were sometimes confused by railroad commuters. So in 1915, Webster Avenue became Kirkwood Road. The sections north and south of Kirkwood remained Denny Road.

Charles Lindbergh became a hero in 1927 following his historic nonstop flight across the Atlantic Ocean. City officials wanted to recognize his St. Louis connection, so in 1930 the Denny Road sections became Lindbergh Boulevard. But some residents were unhappy. A group fought unsuccessfully to have the Denny name reinstated. "Or so the story goes," says Burkett.

And you've heard of Route 66, but what about Route 366?

In 1979, US Route 66, America's Mother Road and the connection between the East and West Coasts, was decertified between Joplin, Missouri, and Chicago, Illinois. The Missouri Department of Transportation then became responsible for

upkeep of the Show-Me State's share of the roadway. After modifications and rerouting, the roadway was renamed Missouri Route 366. And to add to the confusion, sections of Route 366 passing through St. Louis were known locally as Chippewa Street and Watson Road.

Street name changes are not uncommon here and elsewhere, Burkett says. "Street name con-figurations change in many areas due to societal conventions and expansion."

Why are there so many one-way streets in St. Louis?

St. Louis streets trace their origins back to Pierre Laclede and the settlers who established a village here in the 1760s. "This settlement will become one of the finest cities in America," Laclede predicted.

Early structures, including a fur trading house, were located near the river on land that's now part of the Gateway Arch grounds. The trading house became the center of the village and the origination point from which all measurements were taken for locating lot divisions and streets. The village initially contained three north-south and three narrower east-west streets (dirt lanes) measuring thirty to thirty-six feet across.

Decades passed, and true to Laclede's prediction, the city grew and expanded. Additional lots, common fields, and streets were measured off as the town plat grew to

STREET TALK

accommodate the increasing population. Old city maps show that most streets measured sixty feet right-of-way.

Once automobiles replaced wagons and streetcars, the streets became too narrow to safely accommodate two-way traffic. In 1923, bond issue funds were approved to help spruce up downtown St. Louis. Many of the narrow streets were converted to one-way traffic. Major thoroughfares like Olive and Market Streets were widened to accommodate multiple traffic lanes.

Street changes have been made in conjunction with construction of new stadiums and the convention center, but little else has changed with St. Louis street configurations.

What's in a name?

Want to understand why certain names were given to streets and sections of St. Louis? Take a look at history books, said noted historian Norbury L. Wayman of the St. Louis Community Development Agency.

In 1826, St. Louis adopted a street-naming system originated by the city of Philadelphia. North-south streets were given number names. East-west streets were named for trees.

The century progressed and the St. Louis population grew. Additional land was platted and development spread from the original downtown village. Streets often were named for land owners or prominent St. Louisans. Henry Shaw's gift of land for a botanical garden resulted in street names such as Shaw, Flora, Botanical, and Tower Grove. Other street names utilized during that time read like a Who's Who of St. Louis. Geyer, Russell, LaSalle, and Lafayette honor notable St. Louis residents or historic figures. State names as well as the names of US presidents and Indian tribes were popular street name choices.

 **STREET TALK**

Time passes. Some street names have been changed to recognize achievements of more contemporary individuals or the rich cultural heritage of immigrant populations. But names like Bremen, DeBaliviere, Wells, Baden, Kenrick, Bevo, Marquette, Shenandoah, Bellefontaine, Vandeventer, Bissell, and Cherokee harken back to people and places of yesteryear.

Fact Box

Anti-German sentiment ran high during World War I. St. Louis, with its large German population, wasn't exempt. In the name of patriotism, street names with German origins were changed here and in other large cities. Von Versen Avenue became Enright Avenue, Kaiser Street became Gresham, and Berlin Avenue became Pershing Avenue (in honor of Missouri-born general John Pershing). In recent years, individuals affiliated with German American heritage groups have placed commemorative signs on some streets noting their original names.

PARKING FOR GERMANS ONLY

ALL OTHERS WILL BE TOWED

CITY ORD. 1145

HAMBURG AVE

Urban blight becomes eclectic delight.

Rebirth of the University City Loop

Sometimes it takes just one person with a vision to get things moving. Such was the case with entrepreneur Joe Edwards, the pony-tailed pied piper of University City.

Edwards returned to STL, his hometown, after college. He and his wife, Linda, decided to open a small music-themed restaurant/ bar along Delmar Boulevard in the part of University City called the Loop. The Loop was a shopping and entertainment mecca in the first half of the twentieth century but fell out of favor as suburbia crept further west from downtown St. Louis.

Edwards quickly determined that his business wouldn't be successful unless the Loop area changed for the better. So began his one-man campaign to renew and rejuvenate an area that had once been vital. Original buildings with graceful architectural details remained. The area just needed some TLC and for others to see the economic potential. So Edwards got to work, forming committees to address things like lighting, sanitation, and security.

STREET TALK

Blueberry Hill Restaurant became a popular destination. The food was great, the beer cold, and the live entertainment excellent. Plus Edwards's amazing collection of ephemera and items from his childhood spoke to the memories of people throughout the St. Louis area.

In the 1980s, he created another attraction outside Blueberry Hill, the St. Louis Walk of Fame. Patterned after the Hollywood Walk of Fame, STL's walk has expanded to both sides of the street and pays homage to more than 140 famous St. Louisans.

And the revitalization continued. In 1995, Edwards bought and restored the nearby Tivoli Theater, which dated back to 1924. In 2000, he opened the Pageant, a performance venue. He opened Pin-Up Bowl in 2003 and the Moonrise Hotel, a boutique luxury hotel, in 2009. His latest projects include the Peacock Loop Diner and the 2.2-mile track trolley that connects the Loop to STL's crown jewel, Forest Park.

Gradually businesses and consumers returned to University City. Today the Loop is a destination for shopping, dining, and relaxing. Boutiques, unique shops, and local restaurants fill the once-vacant storefronts. Outdoor dining and street performers add to the ambiance of this thriving area. And it all started with the vision of one person.

Fact BOX

A visit to Blueberry Hill isn't complete without a quick peek at Joe Edwards's celebrity photograph walls. Here can be found images of the famous and infamous who've stopped to visit the Loop's most popular man. And if you're really lucky, you might catch a glimpse of rock and roll legend Chuck Berry, who lives near St. Louis and performs regularly at Blueberry Hill.

Do you
believe in
ghosts?

Maybe you've seen them. Drive through St. Louis and notice the walls of some of the city's old brick buildings. They may be faded and difficult to decipher, but they're there. Before the days of billboards and neon and electric signs, advertisements were painted on the exterior walls of buildings. These faded but still somewhat visible images today are called ghost signs, and they're remnants of early St. Louis outdoor advertising.

Nineteenth-century businesspeople were savvy. Businesses were flexing their marketing muscles and stretching advertising dollars more than a century ago. They realized that not just any building would do. High visibility was important. Advertising signs were painted on buildings thought to have the greatest pedestrian, carriage, train, and later automobile traffic.

The more times the advertisements were seen, the better and more cost-effective the advertisements.

In reality, the businesspeople paying to have the products and services advertised on building walls probably had something temporary in mind. They might be amazed that the bold letters and graphics advertising things like flour, tobacco, buggies, stove polish, patent medicines, and beverages would still be visible more than a hundred years later. Such was the advantage of yesteryear's lead-based paints.

Individuals who painted wall advertisements were called walldogs. This was before OSHA regulations regarding workplace hazards, safety equipment, and eight-hour workdays. Walldogs worked tirelessly from the tops of ladders while juggling paint cans and brushes. They were artists whose skills were in demand as they traveled throughout the country.

Perhaps nineteenth-century wall advertising wasn't such a novel idea. Humans have been drawing and painting on cave walls throughout the world for tens of thousands of years!

Soulard Farmers Market

Something for SOULARD FARMER'S MARKET SINCE 1779 **everyone**

It's difficult to describe Soulard Farmers Market. It's a good place to get fresh meat, produce, and gourmet coffee on weekdays. It's a hopping place for the unusual to the sublime on summer weekends. It's been a mainstay on Carroll Street since widow Julia Soulard donated land for a market in 1838. But it's so much more than a large brick building and open-air stalls. Let's just say it's a place you have to visit to understand.

🏛 **TREASURES**

See the colorful rows of fresh and organic fruits and vegetables (most vendors offer samples!). Hear vendors calling out the day's meat specials (including alligator) or a country blues trio doing their funky version of "You Are My Sunshine." Smell the fresh roasted nuts and exotic spices. Taste samples of cheese and local honey. Touch the details of hand-crafted jewelry and apparel or the soft fur of live domestic animals. Soulard Farmers Market is a place to be experienced with all five senses.

The market is open year-round, Wednesday through Sunday. Some vendors, like Schweiger's Produce, have been selling at the market for generations. Other vendors are newcomers to the market scene.

Stay an hour. Stay all day. There's plenty to see, do, eat, and drink at Soulard Farmers Market, including live music performers at each end and a band in the middle, a pocket park, fresh mini-donuts, and a full range of cocktails on Saturday morning. Even if you don't plan to buy the quail eggs, chances are you'll want to bring cash and a few shopping bags for those other items you discover that you simply can't live without! Don't forget to try the barbecue place across the street (the line forms early) or to wander the Soulard neighborhood shops after you've filled the car cooler with hand-picked farm products.

How did so many museums end up so close to each other?

The Metropolitan Zoological Park and Museum District was established to oversee the tax-supported finances of five top-notch St. Louis cultural institutions: the Saint Louis Zoo, the Saint Louis Art Museum, the Saint Louis Science Center, the Missouri Botanical Garden, and the Missouri History Museum.

Establishment of the Zoo–Museum District (ZMD) in 1972 was an affirmation of support by citizens of both the city of St. Louis and St. Louis County, a guarantee that these institutions will continue to provide enriching experiences for residents and visitors both now and in the future. "I think the Zoo–Museum District is very effective," says Robert Lowery Sr., one of eight ZMD commissioners.

"It works for St. Louis and St. Louis County. We have five of the finest venues in the country in St. Louis."

Four of the five institutions are located in Forest Park. The Missouri Botanical Garden is located a few miles south of Forest Park. And the best thing about them? Free or minimal admission for everyone!

City Museum

One person's trash is another's treasure.

There's a place in St. Louis where the building never stops. A place where items once thought to be trash have been functionally repurposed. A place so unique, so quirky, and oh so much fun for all ages. Welcome to the City Museum!

Artist Bob Cassilly had the idea for a one-of-a-kind museum filled with architectural cast-offs and reclaimed visual oddities collected throughout St. Louis. And because some of the items he collected were huge (think airplanes, a log cabin, bridges, and a school bus), he needed plenty of room for visitors to play and explore. With the help of additional artists, he began construction of a museum like no other. In 1997, he opened the City Museum in part of a former shoe warehouse with more than six hundred thousand square feet.

The City Museum continues to grow and expand. A skate park, a Ferris wheel, a series of man-made caves, and miles of mosaics add to the fun. MonstroCity and the museum's rooftop provide places to explore as well as catch fabulous elevated views of downtown St. Louis.

This **ZOO** is a pretty big deal, isn't it?

St. Louis's world-class zoo

Lions, tigers, and bears. Fish, reptiles, and insects. The ninety-acre Saint Louis Zoo is home to more than 560 species of animals, some rare and endangered. But it's not just the animals and state-of-the-art exhibits that make it a world-class zoo. "We work in conjunction with about 180 zoo partners and conservation organizations to focus on assessing animal health, sustaining habitats, wildlife management, breeding endangered species, education, and research," says Susan Gallagher, director of public relations for the Saint Louis Zoo.

According to Gallagher, establishing a zoological park in Forest Park was a lengthy process. Forest Park opened in 1876. A small collection of animals from the city's Fairground Park was purchased in 1891. In 1904, a domed walk-through flight cage was built by the Smithsonian Institution for the World's Fair. The cage was to be disassembled, but it was so popular that the city of St. Louis bought it in 1905 for $3,500.

TREASURES

In 1910, citizens organized the Zoological Society of St. Louis. The city set aside seventy-seven acres for a zoological park in Forest Park in 1913 and established a Zoological Board of Control. The society incorporated as an independent civic organization in 1914. In 1916, citizens voted to tax themselves to pay for construction of the Saint Louis Zoo, becoming the first city in the world to do so.

"St. Louis has the unique distinction of being one of only three accredited zoos in the world that is free for everyone," says Gallagher. "It was created for St. Louisans by St. Louisans."

The Saint Louis Zoo has more than 18,700 wild animals, including thousands of ants, butterflies, and leafcutters. The zoo has 330 full-time employees and approximately 800 seasonal part-time employees to care for its residents. Each year the zoo attracts three million visitors.

Does that building really mean no harm to our planet?

James S. McDonnell Planetarium at the Saint Louis Science Center

To some, it's that building near the zoo resembling a spaceship. Others notice the huge bow and colored lights during the holidays. In reality, it's the James S. McDonnell Planetarium, part of the Saint Louis Science Center.

TREASURES

The Planetarium dates to the early 1960s when space exploration was a hot topic. St. Louis's McDonnell Aircraft, important in the manufacture of the *Mercury* and *Gemini* space capsules, provided finances to construct a center for learning about and observing space. Famed local architect Gyo Obata designed the hyperboloid structure that opened to the public in 1963.

"It's a great resource for the city," says Bill Kelly, senior educator at the Planetarium. "It's a place for enthusiasts to learn more about astronomy. Schools can use visits here to supplement science curriculum. We have presentations about the night sky, constellations, galaxies, Mars, and the solar system. Plus our theater gives a very realistic night-sky experience."

The Planetarium, once owned by the city of St. Louis, was sold to the Saint Louis Science Center in the 1980s. A new science center opened in 1991 and featured a glass bridge over the highway to connect the two buildings.

Public nighttime sky watching is held every first Friday of the month in conjunction with the St. Louis Astronomical Society. "We bring out portable telescopes, and with the curvature of the Planetarium's roof, a lot of the artificial light from the city is cut out," Kelly says. "People can come, ask questions, and learn. We have about 150–200 in attendance, even on cold nights.

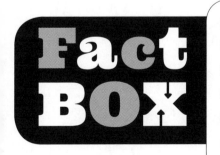

Fact BOX

Gyo Obato graduated from Washington University. His designs can be seen throughout the world and in numerous St. Louis office buildings. He designed the Saint Louis Zoo's Children's Zoo and Living World and was involved with the renovation of Union Station.

What's that building that looks like a cross between a bird's nest and a jungle gym?

The Climatron, a unique St. Louis structural gem

Buckminster Fuller was a twentieth-century inventor and innovator. The introduction of his unique geodesic dome structures in the 1950s generated much interest. With Fuller's dome design in mind, the Missouri Botanical Garden set out to build a greenhouse with no interior supports. It would be the first use of Fuller's design as a greenhouse and its construction would coincide with the garden's 100th anniversary.

🏛 TREASURES

"The Missouri Botanical Garden was trying to look to the future, to find a new symbol for the second hundred years," says Missouri Botanical Garden archivist Andrew Colligan. "The goal was to capture the public's imagination."

The Climatron's dome was built of Plexiglas and was intended to last five to ten years. It successfully attracted attention, but it leaked from the beginning. Renovations began in 1988 and included replacing the ½"-thick Plexiglas with ¾"-thick tempered glass. The new panes were heavier, so an exoskeleton was built above the existing structure to support the additional weight. The Plexiglas was then removed.

"None of the other Fuller-inspired domes in the US are exactly like this one," says Colligan. "It was the first of its kind and the only dome in the St. Louis area."

Fact BOX

"Attendance at the garden was down in the 1950s because nothing was new," says Missouri Botanical Garden archivist Andrew Colligan. "The space industry started up at this time, and the dome looked like it was from outer space. There was no admission fee then for the garden. The Climatron opened in October 1960 with a fifty cents per person admission fee, and attendance soared. Twice as many visitors (four hundred thousand) came to the garden that year, even with the admission charge. It was a shot in the arm. It turned the garden around financially with the new funding generated by the dome."

Singing
the Blues

St. Louis is home to some amazing cultural and civic institutions. The April 2016 opening of the National Blues Museum downtown marked the addition of another cultural gem, this one recognizing the American music form known as the Blues.

Blues music has roots in social and economic oppression, hard times, and love gone wrong. It is unique in that it doesn't follow traditional musical form and expresses raw emotion in its beats and lyrics. The late singer Ray Charles once said, "Everybody can understand the Blues!"

"This is the only Blues museum dedicated to telling the story of the Blues locally, nationally, and internationally," says museum spokesperson Jacqueline Dace. "The goal is for the museum to be the premier entertainment educational resource focusing on the Blues as the foundation of American music."

Some Blues historians believe the blues originated in the Mississippi Delta and followed the mass migration of African Americans north after the Civil War. Many of those who left the area settled or performed in St. Louis as they headed north, bringing their unique music form with them. Composer W. C. Handy is credited with popularizing Blues music. He wrote the song "St. Louis Blues"

TREASURES

in 1914 and said, "The Blues come from want, from desire, longing." Most American music forms introduced since then, including rock and roll, trace their origins to the Blues.

The National Blues Museum has been in the works for several years. It includes a performance area for musicians called the Lumiere Place Legends Room, where limited-engagement shows will be scheduled. An item of interest currently at the museum is a loaned guitar, an original Lucille, from the B. B. King Museum in Indianola, Mississippi.

Fact BOX

St. Louis was the home of innovative Blues style in the 1920s. Noted Blues musicians of that era included Lonnie Johnson, Henry Townsend, and female vocalists Eva Taylor and Alice Moore. More recent St. Louis Blues musicians include Miles Davis, Tina Turner, and Fontella Bass.

A big stainless steel parabola

The Gateway Arch

It was 1948. The city of St. Louis wanted to recognize Thomas Jefferson's part in the historic Louisiana Purchase and the city's role as the gateway to westward expansion in the US. A competition was announced for the design of a symbolic monument to be built in downtown St. Louis.

A design submitted by Finnish-born, American-educated architect Eero Saarinen was selected. Sleek and unadorned, his design was symbolic of the city's place as the starting point for settlers headed west. When completed, the inverted stainless-steel catenary curve or arch would stand 630 feet high, more than twice the height of the Statue of Liberty, and would overlook the mighty Mississippi River.

But construction did not begin for years. Unfortunately, Saarinen died in 1961 before the monument was built. His office supervised the construction that was completed in October 1965.

The Arch is a modern marvel. Foundations for its two legs were placed sixty feet into the ground, and the stainless-steel frame was designed to withstand strong winds as well as earthquakes. Small elevator cars carry visitors to the top of the monument and its observation windows. Routine cleaning of the Arch's exterior keeps it looking bright and shiny for the millions of visitors it welcomes annually.

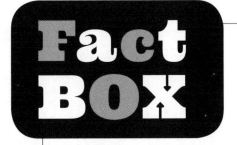

Fact BOX

Eero Saarinen had a connection to another modern architectural marvel— the spectacular Sydney Opera House. A selection jury for the Opera House commission discarded several designs, including one submitted by architect Jorn Utzon. Saarinen looked through the discarded designs, recognized the merit in Utzon's unique design, and convinced the jury to select it. Saarinen also designed Washington, D.C.'s Dulles International Airport and the iconic Tulip chair.

A Witness to History

The Old Courthouse

If walls could talk, those of the Old Courthouse near the riverfront could fill volumes.

The building began its life in 1826, a time when St. Louis's population was less than five thousand. It was known as the County Courthouse for fifty years before the city of St. Louis and St. Louis County became separate entities.

For many decades, the building—and later its signature dome—stood out in the downtown skyline. Today the building is dwarfed by surrounding commercial and residential structures. It and the Basilica of Saint Louis, King of France (a.k.a. the Old Cathedral) stand as visible reminders of St. Louis as it once was. These properties, along with the Gateway Arch and its surrounding property, comprise the US National Park Service's Jefferson National Expansion Memorial.

Most significant of the countless historic moments at the courthouse were the trials of Dred Scott and his wife, Harriet, who sued for freedom from enslavement in 1847 and 1850. A decision was eventually handed down by the US Supreme Court. These actions helped people form strong opinions about slavery in the US, ultimately leading to the Civil War.

The Old Courthouse is open for tours that include its beautifully painted dome ceiling and restored courtrooms.

Why is that symbol everywhere?

Fleur-de-lis, remnants of St. Louis's French connection

It's that three-pronged, flower-looking thing that looks like a Boy Scout symbol. You've probably seen it around St. Louis. It graces everything from street signs and company logos to private-school paraphernalia. So what exactly is it and why is it displayed all over town?

This widely used symbol is called the fleur-de-lis (that's French for "flower of the lily"), and it's a visible remnant of St. Louis's founding by French settlers Pierre Laclede and August Chouteau.

HISTORIC INFLUENCES

Traditional use of the symbol dates back centuries to represent French royalty. It later was used to symbolize French land claims and for decorative purposes.

Surprisingly, despite its religious symbolism, you won't find the fleur-de-lis on display in many of the churches in the Archdiocese of St. Louis, the overseeing organization of the Catholic Church in the city and ten nearby counties. "While the fleur-de-lis is not an official Catholic symbol, we definitely know what it means," says archdiocese spokesperson Gabe Jones. "The lily represents the Virgin Mary. The flower's three petals symbolize the Holy Trinity—Father, Son, and Holy Spirit."

So it's a multipronged symbol used to represent political, artistic, dynastic, scholastic, and sometimes religious enterprises in St. Louis. Gotta love a multitasker!

Fact BOX

The flag of the city of St. Louis features wavy blue lines that meet at a fleur-de-lis. This represents the confluence of the two mighty rivers (Mississippi and Missouri) near an early French settlement—the area that became St. Louis. Many St. Louisans are proud of that French heritage, thus the fleur-de-lis appears frequently.

Why do so many streets have French names . . . that are pronounced incorrectly?

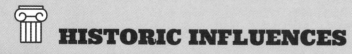

The Mississippi River village that came to be known as St. Louis was settled by Pierre Laclede, Auguste Chouteau, and others of French descent. The tiny settlement had three east-west streets and three north-south streets. Naturally the settlers gave them French names.

In 1809, the original street names were changed to English alphabetical letter names, number names, and tree names. Streets were added as the village grew into a city and followed these naming patterns. As time passed, some newer streets were given the French names of the early village pioneers.

Speculation about the mispronunciation of French street names points to two possibilities: Some guess that people of French descent remained angry years after the French Revolution and intentionally mispronounced French words as a type of rebellion. Others surmised that immigrants settling here from countries like Germany simply didn't know how to correctly pronounce the French names. The mispronunciations became part of the vernacular and have passed from generation to generation.

Was the Civil War a big deal in St. Louis?

STL's importance during the war

JEFFERSON BARRACKS, ST. LOUIS, MO.—LATELY THE SCENE OF GREAT EXCITEMENT ON THE DEPARTURE OF THE FOURTH REGIMENT OF MISSOURI VOLUNTEERS TO TAKE POSSESSION OF BIRD'S POINT, MO.,
OPPOSITE CAIRO, ILL.—FROM A SKETCH BY OUR ARTIST ACCOMPANYING GENERAL LYON'S COMMAND.—SEE PAGE 101.

Missouri was occupied by the Union throughout the war and
pro-Union sentiment was strong, but it was also home to Southern
sympathizers.

HISTORIC INFLUENCES

History books often overlook the contributions of St. Louis and its citizens. "St. Louis was one of the most important transportation, medical, and training centers of the war," says James W. Erwin, author of *The Homefront in Civil War Missouri.* "It was the most important port on the Mississippi River between New Orleans and Minnesota. It was a rail center, and many of the ironclads used by the Union Navy to attack and control the Mississippi, Tennessee, and Cumberland Rivers were built at Carondelet [South St. Louis].

"St. Louis was a major medical center with 15 hospitals and was the headquarters of the Western Sanitary Commission, which provided medical supplies, doctors, and nurses to the Union armies," Erwin continues. "Jefferson Barracks [(South St. Louis)] had a major military hospital and cemetery."

A prison for Confederate civilians, spies, and soldiers was located in St. Louis, as well as a training base for the Union Army. Regiments from Missouri, Illinois, Indiana, Iowa, Wisconsin, Minnesota, and Ohio trained here. The city also had a large horse replacement depot for the cavalry and artillery.

"Where'd you go to high school?" and other St. Louis questions

How St. Louisans categorize each other

UNIQUELY ST. LOUIS

Meet a lifelong St. Louis resident for the first time and you're likely to hear this question: "Where'd you go to high school?"

Doesn't matter how old you are or what part of town you live in now, the question will be asked. So why do St. Louisans ask this question, and why do they care?

"I haven't found a good reason for this question," says *St. Louis Post-Dispatch* columnist and longtime St. Louis resident Joe Holleman. "Is it a class judgment question? Maybe. More likely it has to do with the number of schools, particularly parochial schools, in the St. Louis area.

"At one time there was a higher percentage of kids attending Catholic schools in St. Louis than in any other place in the country. Perhaps the question began years ago as a way to identify if someone was Catholic or not."

So is this question asked in other large cities? "I've not found it in other cities," Holleman says. "I don't think people in other cities focus on the high school question."

Other questions asked by longtime St. Louis residents include:

"Do you live in the city or the county?"
"What part of the county do you live in?"
"What side of the river (insert Mississippi or Missouri) do you live on?"

So why all the questions? Socioeconomic determiners? Status indicators? Stereotyping mechanisms? Personal curiosity? Perhaps all of the above.

I see it's a garage sale, but where's the garage?

The unspoken rules of STL garage sales

St. Louisans love a good garage sale. In STL, "garage sale" is a generic term used to describe for-sale items displayed not only in garages, but also in driveways, yards, basements, the back of pick-up trucks, on sidewalks, and under carports.

Household items, toys, books, clothing, furniture, exercise equipment, athletic equipment, baby items, sports memorabilia, and more. If you're looking for it or collecting it, drive around long enough on a Wednesday or Saturday and you're likely to find it. The earlier in the morning you hit the road, the more likely you are to find treasures.

UNIQUELY ST. LOUIS

Joe Holleman, *St. Louis Post-Dispatch* columnist and expert on all things St. Louis, says he's wondered why garage sales are held only on Wednesdays and Saturdays. "I think it goes back to the days before electronic media, when newspapers carried pages of classified ads and offered discounted advertising rates if you ran an ad on a Wednesday or Saturday."

St. Louis garage sales have a few unspoken rules that you'll only hear from seasoned pickers. These include targeting certain neighborhoods (some have the reputation for offering higher-quality items), cruising these areas well before the standard start time (7 a.m.), taking an ample supply of cash, and bartering for lower prices whenever possible. Also, it's not cool to approach a bathrobe-clad resident strolling to grab the newspaper—even if you can clearly see a sale is about to happen there. If it's not 7 a.m., don't ask for a quick sneak peek.

FYI, according to the St. Louis City Revised Code, Chapter 15.156, Division IX, Miscellaneous Offenses and Regulations: "It shall be unlawful to conduct any sale at retail in the front yard of any residentially zoned property, as the term 'front yard' is herein defined, which said sale is known as a yard sale, garage sale or lawn sale." The penalty for violation (if you're caught) is a fine of "not less than $50.00 nor more than $500.00 or imprisonment for not more than 90 days or both such fine and imprisonment."

St. Louis is called the Mound City. Is it big on desserts?

Ancient civilizations dug St. Louis

The landscape of today's St. Louis looks much different than it did when Frenchmen Pierre Laclede and August Chouteau settled here in the 1700s. At that time, the land was dotted with several dozen enormous mounds thought to have been created by ancient civilizations.

The close proximity to the Mississippi, Missouri, and Illinois Rivers, plus fertile land, made the area an appealing place to settle.

Some guessed the mounds were mass burial sites. Others said they had ceremonial significance and contained relics from daily life.

The mounds became landmarks. River travelers knew they were near St. Louis when they spotted the mounds in the distance. St. Louis acquired the nickname Mound City.

As the city grew during the nineteenth century, the mounds were leveled and built over. Dirt from the mounds was used in the production of bricks and as fill during railroad construction.

Today only one large mound remains in St. Louis. Sugarloaf Mound, located south of downtown on a bluff overlooking the Mississippi River, most likely survived thanks to a house built on its peak decades ago. The Osage Nation now owns the property and plans to preserve it as a sacred site.

Several area businesses include Mound City in their names, but the reference is to the earthen mounds once found here, not the candy.

Why is that guy Ted Drewes so popular? Is he giving away bags of money?

Say the name "Ted Drewes" to any St. Louisan and you'll likely see a big grin. Ted is just that well known. Generations of St. Louis families have grown up enjoying the sweet, creamy goodness of Ted's frozen custard. It's like a rite of passage.

Drive down Chippewa Street (one of two locations) on a warm evening and you're likely to witness the Ted Drewes phenomenon—long lines, slow traffic, street-party atmosphere. Most customers stop for a frozen custard concoction called a concrete. (FYI, the consistency is so thick that servers prove it by turning it upside down before handing it to customers—and the contents stay put!)

 **UNIQUELY ST. LOUIS**

It all started with Ted Drewes Sr. He didn't invent frozen custard, but he introduced it to St. Louis in 1930. The automobile industry was young and quickly becoming mobile. Ted set up stands in several St. Louis locations before opening one along what became US Route 66 (today's Chippewa Street)—the Mother Road. And so began a St. Louis tradition.

Ted Jr. runs the business started by his father. "It really is good, guys and gals!" he says. But he isn't the only frozen custard vendor in town. Others include Fritz's, Andy's, and Mr. Wizard's. Customers say the custard taste varies according to each establishment's unique recipe (some say honey is the secret ingredient).

Another thing you'll find at Ted Drewes and the other frozen custard stands is socialization—the chance to mix and mingle with friends, neighbors, pets, and even strangers. It's a tradition St. Louisans embrace.

What sayeth the Veiled Prophet?
And doeth we care?

St. Louis and its storied traditions

Maybe it was a quaint fairy tale. Or maybe it wasn't.

Throughout its history, St. Louis has been a city of distinct socioeconomic classes with racial and gender disparities. An elite group of people ran the city.

Uprisings by working-class St. Louisans in the 1870s were a cause of concern to the city fathers. In response, those in positions of social and political authority devised a secret society that in 1878 hosted what became an annual fable-like pageant and parade to entertain the masses and at the same time send a message.

 **UNIQUELY ST. LOUIS**

The message was that the elite control the city and will continue to do so even if armed action is necessary. The message was conveyed in the persona of the Veiled Prophet from the Kingdom of Khorassan, a.k.a. the Grand Oracle. His head covering and clothing resembled that of Klansmen. He was accompanied by costumed assistants bearing weapons.

In addition, each year a Queen of Love and Beauty (daughter of one of the VP members) was selected by the organization to "rule" over a ball (debutante gathering).

Many St. Louisans were enthralled by the lavish show of wealth parading through the city streets each year. They embraced the mythical story and attended VP events by the tens of thousands. Others saw it as a flaunting of elitist wealth.

"The organization, through the parade and ball it sponsored, made the members feel like good fathers both to the city and to their own daughters," says Dr. Thomas M. Spencer, director of honors student affairs at Eastern Illinois University and author of *The St. Louis Veiled Prophet Celebration—Power on Parade, 1877–1995.* "The increased trade during the St. Louis Fair helped the city, thus making these men feel they were being good city fathers. The success of the Veiled Prophet ball in giving their daughters a 'night to remember,' as well as helping the daughters find good marriage prospects, made them feel they were being good fathers in the usual sense."

Television brought increased attention to the VP festivities, but the mid-twentieth century's growing civil rights movement brought about a steep decline in their popularity. In recent years the Veiled Prophet organization has become more diverse and inclusive. It has adopted a more community-minded philosophy and assists with the city's Independence Day celebration.

Here's to your health!

St. Louis hospitals offer hope and healing.

Big cities have strengths and weaknesses. Something St. Louis does, and does really well, is health care.

Washington University and Saint Louis University have renowned medical schools and multiple hospital affiliations. Barnes-Jewish College of Nursing traces its roots to 1905.

SSM Health is headquartered in St. Louis and is one of the largest Catholic healthcare systems in the United States. It has affiliate operations in four states.

BJC Health Systems has a lengthy history dating to the 1890s and includes the combined resources and expertise of what once were three separate hospital systems—Barnes Hospital, Jewish Hospital, and Christian Health Services. Numerous medical "firsts" have happened at these hospitals, including the use of gloves in operating rooms, installation of an electronic data processing system in a hospital, and nerve transplants. St. Louis medical professionals also have been leaders in laparoscopic surgery and in vitro fertilization.

St. Louis Children's Hospital dates to 1879. It was the first children's hospital west of the Mississippi River and was founded by eight women. The hospital provides pediatric services to children from around the world. Among its specialties are the treatment of cerebral palsy, cleft palate, epilepsy, and bone marrow and liver transplants.

Public parks both large and small

St. Louis loves its public parks! They serve as neighborhood anchors, providing needed greenspace where adults and children can gather for recreation and socialization.

The city of St. Louis has 110 parks encompassing more than three thousand acres. St. Louisans' appreciation of their public spaces dates to the city's early days when French settlers brought the custom of setting aside common fields for community gardens. From these developed the city's parks both large and small.

Forest Park (1,293 acres) was established in 1876 and is one of the nation's largest urban parks. It hosted the 1904 World's Fair and is home to the Saint Louis Zoo, Saint Louis Art Museum, Missouri History Museum, and the Muny (oldest and the largest outdoor musical theater in the US).

URBAN OASES

Dan Skillman, commissioner of parks for the city of St. Louis, names Forest Park as his favorite but finds Lafayette Park one of the city's most interesting. "It has great Victorian features and is one of the only parks with a wrought iron fence around it," he says. "It has hidden features, grotto areas, lakes, and strolling areas."

Fact BOX

St. Louis's oldest parks (Gravois, Laclede, and Mount Pleasant) date to 1812. The newest, Chouteau Park and Taylor Park, opened in 2007 and 2008. From the large and lavishly landscaped (Forest Park and Tower Grove) to half-acre Minnesota and Hill Park, each is unique. The parks and forestry departments employ 200 full-time and 150 seasonal employees, including an arborist.

Grant's Farm

THE HOME OF GENERAL GRANT.
ST. LOUIS COUNTY MO

URBAN OASES

Head southwest down Gravois Road and you can't miss it. It's the long stretch of undeveloped bucolic greenspace on the right. And no, your eyes aren't deceiving you: those are indeed American bison, antelope, and zebra grazing contentedly as traffic zooms by. Welcome to Grant's Farm, St. Louis's other animal kingdom.

Grant's Farm once belonged to President and Mrs. Ulysses S. Grant (the couple's rustic cabin remains on the property). In 1903, Adolphus Busch of Anheuser-Busch fame built a sprawling German-style country home and barn for his son, August A. Busch Sr.

Time passed. Soon a menagerie of animals representing more than one hundred species from around the world became Grant's Farm residents along with Busch family members. Beginning in 1954, August A. "Gussie" Busch Jr. opened parts of the farm to tourists and guests. Then, as now, admission is free.

Grant's Farm is open to the public from spring until fall. It attracts more than six hundred thousand visitors annually.

Fact BOX

Budweiser Clydesdales, the large draught horses long identified with Anheuser-Busch products, live and are bred on the grounds of Grant's Farm. Clydesdales also live on-site at the St. Louis brewery. Each hitch horse daily consumes more than twenty quarts of whole grains and vitamins, more than fifty pounds of hay, and as much as thirty gallons of water.

I see dead people.
With cool headstones.

**Bellefontaine and Calvary Cemeteries—
where the in-crowd spends eternity.**

No matter life's successes, everybody dies. And where but cemeteries do the famous and nameless come together?

St. Louis was the gateway to the west in 1849. With a nod to its French founders, it followed a Parisian trend, the Rural Cemetery Movement, establishing cities of the dead far from downtown. The first was Bellefontaine Cemetery, an artistically designed 314-acre parcel located northwest of town.

URBAN OASES

In 1854, Calvary Cemetery was established when the Roman Catholic Archdiocese of St. Louis purchased 470 acres alongside Bellefontaine Cemetery. Then, as now, St. Louisans liked to do things in a *big* way. "We became among the largest cemetery providers in the state," says Calvary Cemetery counselor Matt DeWitt. "You can actually see the history of St. Louis unfold here."

Elaborate stone mausoleums, statues, and markers stand as perpetual monuments to the thousands buried in both cemeteries. And Bellefontaine, also an arboretum, shares its beauty with the living, hosting weddings, runs, and tours. "Visitors can connect names with family history as well as city and US history," says Richard Lay, vice president of Bellefontaine's cemetery association.

With more than eighty-seven thousand gravesites, Bellefontaine is less than half full. Calvary, too, has plenty of room for more.

Fact BOX

The remains of explorer William Clark, author Sara Teasdale, beer baron Adolphus Busch, and kindergarten originator Susan Blow are interred at Bellefontaine Cemetery. Calvary notables include authors Kate Chopin and Tennessee Williams, former slave Dred Scott, and Civil War general William Tecumseh Sherman. Generations of St. Louis's founding families have found their final resting places in these cemeteries.

WILLIAM CLARK
BORN IN VIRGINIA
AUGUST 1, 1770
ENTERED INTO LIFE ETERNAL
SEPTEMBER 1, 1838
SOLDIER, EXPLORER,
STATESMAN AND PATRIOT
HIS LIFE IS WRITTEN

Is Cardinal Nation a religious group?

Almost. St. Louis has baseball fever.

The arrival of spring means one thing to St. Louis Cardinals fans—the start of Major League Baseball!

Some people call Cardinals fanaticism Redbird Fever. Others refer to the thousands of loyal Cardinals baseball fans as Cardinal Nation. Whatever they're called, fans of the National League's St. Louis Cardinals welcome spring and opening day at Busch Stadium with frenzied enthusiasm.

Cardinals Nation also is the name of a venue at Ballpark Village, a sports-centered entertainment area where loyal fans gather to support the Redbirds on game days and throughout the year. Today Busch Stadium encompasses twenty-eight acres

SPORTS

(a whopping 1,270,000 square feet!), including Ballpark Village and seating for approximately 45,000 fans.

Attending a game at Busch Stadium is an experience like no other. The sights and sounds, as well as the tastes and smells, have entertained generations of Redbird fans. And postseason playoff games are memories in the making for St. Louis baseball fanatics.

Fact BOX

Established in 1882, the St. Louis Cardinals have a colorful history. Some of baseball's greatest players have worn Redbird jerseys, including Stan Musial, Dizzy Dean, Lou Brock, Ozzie Smith, and Bob Gibson. The Cardinals' Branch Rickey is credited with developing baseball's farm system. The Cardinals have won eleven World Series championships and nineteen National League pennants, making them one of baseball's most successful teams.

The St. Louis Blues are more than just a hockey team.

STL and its Blue Note fans

Anyone who's attended a St. Louis Blues hockey game knows it's a memorable experience. St. Louis Blues fans are faithful and dedicated followers of the Note. While the Blues have never won the Stanley Cup (the National Hockey League's championship trophy), the team's loyal fans have flocked to arenas to cheer on "the boys" since the team first came to town in 1967.

"I think the key to the St. Louis Blues' huge following is the fact that the ownership is local," says a source with the St. Louis Blues Hockey Club. "The owners appreciate the fans and the pride St. Louis has in the team." Home hockey games draw eighteen to nineteen thousand fans, with tickets for weekend games often in short supply. Frequent promotional giveaway nights enable fans to collect one-of-a-kind souvenirs and collectibles.

"It's been interesting to see how the game of hockey has evolved in the last fifty years here," says the Blues source. "Today the players focus on strength training and safety. In the past, players didn't wear masks and helmets."

Fact BOX

St. Louis Blues hockey games are played at the Scottrade Center, home of the Note since 1995. Home games include regular features like appearances by Louie, the team's mascot; the smooth moves of Zamboni machines between periods; Towel Man (tosses a towel when the team scores); a musical power play ditty complete with hand motions; and repetition of the team's mantra, "Let's Go Blues!" The games are fast-paced and not for the faint of heart. Opposing players sometimes fight and blood hits the ice.

Gone
but not
forgotten

STL's lost sports franchises

Blame it on owner greed, a lack of public interest, or some of both. Whatever the reason, St. Louis has been home to several professional sports teams—at least for a time. These include the St. Louis Hawks and the Spirits of St. Louis, both basketball teams, and two football teams, the St. Louis Cardinals and the St. Louis Rams.

Oh, and there were the years when St. Louis was home to two baseball teams—the St. Louis Browns (American League) and the St. Louis Cardinals (National League). In 1944, both teams battled it out to become baseball's World Series champions. Not to brag, but that was one of eleven times the Cardinals won the World Series.

The St. Louis Hawks played at Kiel Auditorium from 1955 to 1968. The team made it to the National Basketball Association finals four times (1957, 1958, 1960, 1961), winning the NBA championship in 1958.

SPORTS

The Spirits of St. Louis were part of the short-lived American Basketball Association before it merged with the NBA. The Spirits played at the old St. Louis Arena (a.k.a. "the old barn") from 1974 to 1976.

The St. Louis Cardinals football franchise was a part of STL from 1960 to 1987. Sometimes called the Cardiac Cardinals, the team played outdoors at Sportsman's Park/Busch Stadium and the second Busch Stadium. They never won the Super Bowl. After the Cardinals left for Phoenix, it took eight years to bring another National Football League franchise to St. Louis.

The St. Louis Rams arrived in the Gateway City in 1995 amid much fanfare. After a few outdoor games at the second Busch Stadium, the team moved into a new domed stadium in the heart of downtown. The Rams won Super Bowl XXXIV in 1999. They played their last home game in St. Louis in December 2015 before relocating to Los Angeles.

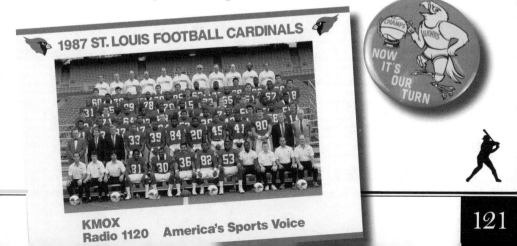

St. Louis Arena

The Old Barn

If walls could talk, those of Oakland Avenue's old St. Louis Arena could have spoken volumes. It was the scene of countless memorable moments in twentieth-century St. Louis history.

The building that came to be known as the Arena was unique when it opened in late September 1929. Its ceiling was supported by twenty cantilevered steel trusses, not upright posts. Built to house the National Dairy Show and livestock shows, only one such show was held there. The October 1929 stock market crash put an end to those plans, and soon the building was for sale.

Through the years, the large structure hosted sporting events, conventions, horse and rodeo shows, ice shows, circuses, and concerts. Then in 1967, businessman Sid Salomon and investors brought professional hockey to the Arena. They called the team the St. Louis Blues.

The Blues quickly garnered a fan base with players like Barclay Plager, Garry Unger, Jacques Plante, and Bernie Federko. In the early days, ticket prices ranged from $2.50 to $6.00, which made it an

SPORTS

affordable sport for many St. Louisans. Home hockey games took on a party atmosphere.

In 1981, the Arena became the Checkerdome when it was purchased by local company Ralston Purina, whose corporate identity included a red and white checkerboard design. By the 1990s, the Arena's days of usefulness were numbered. A larger modern arena was built in the heart of downtown. The Kiel Center, today called Scottrade Center, became the new home of the St. Louis Blues.

But St. Louisans are sentimental. Seats from the old barn were removed and sold prior to the building's implosion in 1999. Today the space is occupied by an office building.

Livin' just enough for the city . . . which is different from living in the county; or City Mouse, County Mouse.

St. Louis City and St. Louis County, a unique municipal arrangement

It probably seemed like a good idea at the time, or so the city fathers thought. In 1877, St. Louis became the first city in the US to enact a home rule city charter. St. Louis City and St. Louis County, which had been one, formally separated. Each established its own government and judicial systems, municipal services, and taxation rates.

City limit boundaries were defined to allow plenty of space for continued growth and expansion in the decades ahead. At least that was the plan. In reality, St. Louis City experienced rapid growth during the 1880s–1890s. Its position as a transportation crossroads attracted industries. Immigrants, particularly from Germany and Italy, flocked here in search of a new life in the Gateway to the West. It wasn't long before the city reached its boundaries. If growth was to continue, and it did, it would be necessary to expand outside the city limits and into St. Louis County. Plus the city could not annex land belonging to the county.

Transportation options and increased popularity of the automobile, coupled with the desire to leave residential crowding and the grit of downtown industries, led thousands to flee to the suburbs of St. Louis County. The result has been population increases in the county and decreases in the city over the last sixty-five years.

Brick, brick everywhere;

or St. Louis 3, Big Bad Wolf 0.

The abundance of brick homes and buildings in STL

Drive through St. Louis and its neighborhoods and you'll notice that sturdy brick structures are everywhere. From residences on quiet, tree-lined streets to low-rise buildings and industrial warehouses near the Mississippi River, brick has long been a popular building material here. "In fact, St. Louis was the largest brick producing city in the world by the turn of the nineteenth century," says Andrew Weil, executive director of the Landmarks Association of St. Louis..

"St. Louis has perfect geology for brick production. A geological feature called the 'Cheltenham Syncline' underlies a lot of southwest St. Louis. It is defined by large quantities of clays that are suitable for building brick and refractory brick, as well as coal to fire them."

St. Louisans probably began making and using soft, low-fired brick for chimneys and ovens in the late 1700s. By the late 1840s, it probably was the dominant building material, says Weil. "By the second half of the nineteenth century, advances in technology led to mass machine production of highly standardized, very dense, very hard hydraulic-pressed brick that was produced by the millions and shipped all over the country." St. Louis's brick production hit its peak in the early twentieth century. And St. Louis–produced brick is still in demand.

It is reused here and also sold all over the country," says Weil.

Why did the Italians seek high ground?

Topography contributed to this STL neighborhood's nickname.

The nineteenth century saw the discovery of large clay deposits beneath much of southwest St. Louis. Landmarks Association of St. Louis executive director Andrew Weil says the clay was suitable for making bricks. It wasn't long before brick production facilities opened in the area.

As the twentieth century approached, European immigrants arrived in St. Louis in search of a new life. Numerous Italians were drawn by the prospects of clay and brick work. Many settled nearby on what was the most elevated ground in St. Louis, an area later dubbed the Hill. Soon St. Louis was the largest brick-producing city in the world.

Clay jobs were plentiful. Workers sent word to their families and friends about the opportunities in St. Louis. Newcomers arrived and settled on the Hill, and the Italian neighborhood grew. They brought with them their food, culture, and a strong sense of community.

WHERE WE LIVE

More than a hundred years later, that close-knit neighborhood bond remains. Many who live on the Hill are lifelong residents, as were their parents and grandparents. The neighborhood's many restaurants feature savory foods prepared using treasured family recipes. It's an epicurean's delight. Benvenuti a St. Louis!

Fact BOX

The Hill's streets are narrow, lined with rows of small, tidy houses and yards. The Hill's unique fire hydrants are painted red, white, and green and resemble the Italian flag.

THE ITALIAN IMMIGRANTS

What's up with all the four-family flats?

WHERE WE LIVE

Cruise the streets of St. Louis and you'll see them. They're the brick residences with multiple front doors. St. Louisans call them flats. Contrary to what some may think, they weren't built by someone who really liked exterior doors. They house multiple family units.

St. Louis was an important industrial city by the late 1800s. Its proximity to the Mississippi and Missouri Rivers, plus its position as a crossroads for multiple railroads, made it an ideal location for business development. Business growth meant the need for additional workers, and workers needed places to live.

"St. Louis was a huge city," says Andrew Weil, executive director of the Landmarks Association of St. Louis. "Flats became popular in middle- and working-class neighborhoods in the early twentieth century where space was at a premium."

Numerous St. Louis streets, particularly south and southwest of downtown, are lined with brick flats. "Often if a family could afford to build a residence, they'd build one with an extra unit for rental, which would provide additional income," says the Landmarks Association's Rick Rosen. "It didn't cost that much more to build a multiple-family dwelling than a single-family home."

Multiple-unit housing can be found in other large cities. "Cleveland, Baltimore, and Cambridge, Massachusetts, have them," says Rosen. "What's unique about St. Louis housing is the amount of flourishes and detail work on even the most modest dwellings. The labor and craftsmanship were highly skilled. The humblest houses resemble palaces in the details and embellishments."

You call these skyscrapers?

St. Louis—a leader in architectural style

St. Louis may not be home to the world's tallest skyscrapers, but the 1891 Louis H. Sullivan–designed ten-story Wainwright Building was the first tall office building of its kind.

"The Wainwright Building was unique in that the exterior masonry was supported by a steel frame," says Rick Rosen of the

WHERE WE LIVE

Landmarks Association of St. Louis. "Height wasn't the goal here. It was the building's vertical aesthetics. The aesthetics expressed that this was a new and different office building. It had very dramatic vertical shafts, with shadow and light demonstrating the tallness of the building, not that it was the tallest building. The Wainwright Building broke completely and cleanly with the architectural trends of the past."

St. Louisan Ellis Wainwright was a wealthy businessman, a patron of great architecture as well as of the modern and unique. Sullivan's fresh ideas were intriguing, so Wainwright secured him to design his St. Louis office building. The result was a structure that pleased Wainwright and earned Sullivan accolades. He was given the unofficial title, "father of modern American architecture."

The Wainwright Building was listed on the National Register of Historic Places in 1968 and today houses state of Missouri offices.

Fact BOX

The thirteen-floor Civil Courts Building on North Tucker Boulevard looks like two distinct buildings—one on top of the other. The top section is a replica of the tomb of King Mausolus (one of the Seven Wonders of the Ancient World) built in Asia Minor in 352 B.C. It features thirty-two Ionic columns (eight on each side) and a pyramid-shaped roof topped with two sphinxlike creatures sporting St. Louis's symbol, the fleur-de-lis. The building was constructed between 1928 and 1930, a time when architects looked to ancient structures for design ideas. The building houses a law library.

Wait . . . you had to leave home to take a bath?

Once upon a time, St. Louis had the fourth-largest US population. It was also a stinky, dirty place. Waste disposal, sanitation, and hygiene were primitive, at best.

Garbage filled ash pits near outdoor privies. Horse manure and animal carcasses littered the streets. Industrialization led to poor air and water quality.

Personal hygiene? Almost nonexistent.

WHERE WE LIVE

Houses had no running water; few had bath tubs. Bathing was an ordeal that required multiple trips to an outdoor water source and heating water over a fire before dumping it into a washtub. If the household included multiple generations, which many did, they often used the same bath water.

In the 1890s, social reformers sought to improve living conditions in large cities, including promoting cleanliness. This led to construction of public bathhouses in several large US cities, but St. Louis was slow to join the public bath movement.

Public Bath House No. 1 opened here in August 1907 with separate facilities for men and women. There was no charge to use the bathhouse, but soap and towels could be rented if not brought from home. The concept was declared a success, with more than five hundred thousand people using the facility by 1915. Five additional bathhouses were built in St. Louis. The last bathhouse, built in 1937, remained open until 1965. It still stands near the popular Crown Candy Kitchen.

The spirit of flight

St. Louis has a long history of involvement with aeronautics. "St. Louis was important to aviation and aviation was important to St. Louis," says attorney and author Alan Hoffman, an advocate for the aviation legacy of St. Louis.

According to Hoffman, St. Louis played a major role in many aviation industry "firsts." St. Louisan Albert Bond Lambert was friends with American and European balloonists and aircraft pioneers, took flying lessons with the famous Wright brothers, and created the earliest St. Louis area airports (St. Louis's current airport bears his name).

Glenn Curtiss made the first flight in St. Louis at Forest Park in October 1909. In 1910, President Theodore Roosevelt came to St. Louis to attend the International Air Tournament. The tournament attracted leading American and foreign aviators and airplane builders. Roosevelt was invited to fly with a young pilot, accepted the invitation on the spot, and became the first US president to fly.

Thomas Benoist, an early aircraft builder, designed and built an airplane in University City in 1910 and opened a flying school at

UP IN THE AIR

Kinloch Field in 1911. In March 1912, Albert Berry made the first parachute descent from an airplane at Jefferson Barracks.

St. Louis was also part of the original transcontinental post office air mail network established in 1920. The city's hosting of the 1923 International Air Races (facilitated by Lambert) attracted a young aviator named Charles Lindbergh, who in 1926 established the air mail route between St. Louis and Chicago. It was here that Lindbergh met local business leaders who eventually sponsored his historic non-stop flight between New York and Paris in 1927. In appreciation, he named his aircraft *The Spirit of St. Louis.*

"St. Louis has been a major aircraft production center since 1927 when the Curtiss-Robertson Company was established at Lambert, becoming the predecessor of Curtiss-Wright, McDonnell Aircraft, McDonnell-Douglas, and Boeing," says Hoffman. "Boeing continues to build the F-15 Eagle, F/A-18 Super Hornet, and EA-18G Growler jet aircraft for the US and its allies."

Fact BOX

Lambert–St. Louis Flying Field opened in 1923. Lambert–St. Louis Municipal Airport was established in 1928. It hired the first air traffic controller, Archie League. Military aviation began here in 1923 with the establishment of a National Guard unit at Lambert. Parts of the *Mercury* and *Gemini* spacecraft were designed and constructed in St. Louis.

My beautiful balloon

St. Louis's love of hot-air balloons

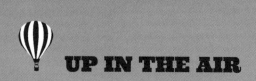

UP IN THE AIR

St. Louis has a long history with hot-air balloons. Beginning in the late 1800s, hot-air balloonists came to St. Louis for demonstrations. Then, as now, the balloons drew crowds of observers.

It's a calm, sunny afternoon in Forest Park, St. Louis's largest urban park. The park's Central Field is alive with noise and activity as crew members inflate more than seventy tethered hot-air balloons. The colorful fabrics unfurl as flames and gasses lift the balloons to an upright position.

Suddenly a single balloon rises above the tree line. Prevailing winds carry the lead balloon and its passengers toward South St. Louis. Soon the other balloons' tethering ropes are released and . . . they're off! The Great Forest Park Balloon Race has begun as it has for the last forty-plus years.

Each September thousands of spectators and certified balloonists from around the country jam Forest Park to witness one of the oldest, biggest, free-of-charge, urban hot-air balloon events.

No two balloons are alike. Some bear colorful corporate identification; others are uniquely shaped. Balloonists attempt to follow the lead balloon and land as close to it as possible when it descends. Spectators young and old love to watch them!

A balloon glow is held in the park the night before the race. It allow spectators to get an up-close look at the nighttime beauty of the lighted, tethered balloons.

This city is fairly infatuated with 1904.

It was 1904 and St. Louis was about to hit the international stage.

After months of negotiating, planning, building, and improving, the Louisiana Purchase Exposition was about to open. Everything from water purification to transportation of people from foreign cultures had been considered. And this was before the days of mass communication and technology. Would the fair begin without a glitch?

"The fair was originally scheduled for 1903 to commemorate the centennial of the Louisiana Purchase, but was delayed to allow more companies and countries to participate," says Max Storm, founder of the 1904 World's Fair Society, Inc. "To get started, the city put up $5 million, the federal government put up $5 million, and fair organizers sold $5 million in fair stock. It was the only world's fair in history that paid for itself."

Washington University, which planned to relocate from downtown to its current site adjacent to Forest Park, delayed moving into thirteen new buildings so the structures could be used during the fair. "Brookings Hall was the fair's administration building," says Storm.

Most of the fair's buildings were designed to be temporary and were removed after the fair. Exceptions were a section of today's Saint Louis Art Museum and the Saint Louis Zoo's Flight Cage, which was a Smithsonian Institution exhibit. The fair closed after seven months and approximately twenty million visitors.

And contrary to popular opinion, hot dogs, ice cream cones, and iced tea were not invented at the fair. "They were popularized at the fair, but not invented there," says Storm. "Puffed rice was introduced at the fair."

Fact BOX

The fair's end was just the beginning of Forest Park, an urban oasis where generations of St. Louisans continue to enjoy beauty and amenities. The admission-free Saint Louis Zoo, Art Museum, and Missouri History Museum attract visitors year-round. The outdoor Municipal Opera (now called the Muny) has been hosting live summer stage performances since it opened in 1919. The Jewel Box, opened in 1936, is a gardener's delight. During winter months, Steinberg Memorial Skating Rink (opened in 1957) attracts ice skating enthusiasts of all ages. When the St. Louis area gets a good blanket of snow, Art Hill, the best sledding hill in town, is dotted with winter enthusiasts riding on everything from snow boards to cafeteria trays. Forest Park has a challenging public golf course, and paved trails around the park host joggers, walkers, and bicyclists each day.

St. Louis really hosted an Olympics?

Hosting the Summer Olympics is a big deal. Countries spend big bucks trying to persuade the Olympic Committee to choose them as the host venue.

Once upon a time (1904 to be exact), the Summer Olympics were hosted in St. Louis. The timing coincided nicely with the World's Fair. It was indeed the year the world came to St. Louis. And the best part was that St. Louis beat out Chicago as the host city.

"The St. Louis Olympics was only the third such modern-day competition," says Max Storm,

THE FAIR

founder of the 1904 World's Fair Society, Inc. "And only four US cities have ever held the Olympics. Chicago wanted the Olympics, had approval to hold it, but St. Louis threatened to overshadow Chicago's games by hosting more events tied to the World's Fair. Chicago decided to let the games be held here."

Several structures remain from the 1904 Olympics and are part of Washington University. The concrete stadium and stands, plus the school's running track, were used during the competition. Parts of a nearby building also were used.

Then as now, there was controversy. The guy who won the marathon cheated. He caught a ride to the finish line and was then disqualified. Thomas Hicks (the true winner) was given strychnine along the way, an accepted practice at that time, to enhance his performance. There were no rules then to prevent such.

Turn right
at the Catholic church.
No, not that one, the other one.

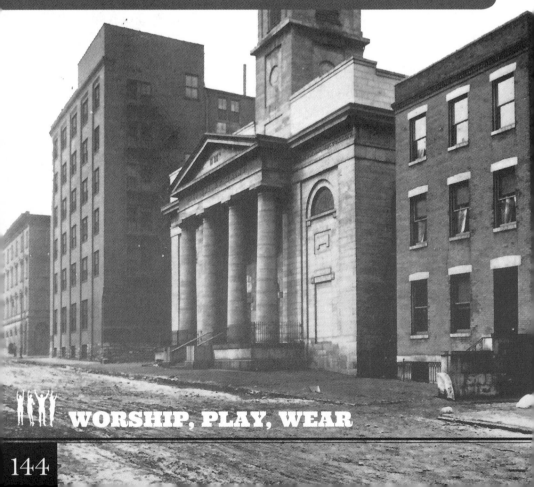

The St. Louis Catholic connection

WORSHIP, PLAY, WEAR

St. Louis founders Pierre Laclede and August Chouteau were of French descent. They also were devout Catholics. Building a house of worship here was a priority. The site they dedicated in 1764 sat near the banks of the Mississippi River.

Today that site still houses a Catholic church (the fourth on the site)—Basilica of Saint Louis, King of France, named in honor of France's King Louis IX. "It was the first Catholic cathedral west of the Mississippi River, is the oldest building in the city of St. Louis, and is the only piece of riverfront property that remains in the hands of its original owner—the Archdiocese of St. Louis," says archdiocese spokesperson Gabe Jones.

And as the population of St. Louis grew and expanded from the original riverfront settlement, so too did the Catholic Church. The St. Louis Archdiocese oversees the operations of the parishes and schools in the city of St. Louis as well as in ten surrounding counties. "The archdiocese has approximately 180 parishes and a network of one-hundred-plus schools," Jones says. "Throughout European history, the French had a profound effect on the Catholic Church. Some of that connection remains in St. Louis."

Fact Box

The Basilica of Saint Louis, King of France, the Parish of St. Louis (a.k.a. the Old Cathedral) was built between 1831 and 1834 with twelve-hundred-pound blocks of granite. And this was long before the invention of bulldozers and forklifts!

This town looks sleepy for a Saturday night.

Some St. Louis neighborhoods come to life after dark.

WORSHIP, PLAY, WEAR

Think St. Louisans roll up the sidewalks after dark? Think again!

St. Louis neighborhoods like the Loop (University City), Washington Avenue (downtown), the Central West End, South Grand Avenue, the Grove (midtown), and Soulard (south city) are self-contained dining and entertainment districts. Restaurants, bars, breweries, theaters, performing venues, and pubs abound. The party's just starting when the sun goes down.

In the mood for something sophisticated? Catch a performance at Powell Symphony Hall, the Fabulous Fox, or the Peabody Opera House.

Thirsty? St. Louis has a dozen breweries both large and small, with selections ranging from wheat brews to lagers. "We market to people who like good beer," says Urban Chestnut's Florian Kuplent.

Want to dance? St. Louis is home to an array of nightclubs where you can dance the night away.

Hungry? St. Louis has a diverse population. One-of-a-kind ethnic restaurants are plentiful and are an epicurean's delight. Or try a pub specializing in authentic Irish food.

Want to listen to smooth jazz or hometown karaoke? St. Louis has both covered at multiple locations.

Need to check on your favorite teams? St. Louis is a sports town and sports bars are plentiful.

How about topping off the night with a dessert martini or a sweet confection? Uptown sophistication or down-home charm, you have choices.

In search of quiet, intimate surroundings or cozy atmosphere? They're here too.

St. Louis nightlife is happening!
Just ask a local for suggestions.

Over 100 years old, but still called new?

Cathedral Basilica of Saint Louis—the New Cathedral

The Catholic Church has been an integral part of St. Louis since its founding in 1764. An early structure erected by the French settlers was a house (actually more of a shed) of worship. That riverfront site today is occupied by the Cathedral Basilica of Saint Louis, King of France, the Parish of St. Louis. Its stately spire is somewhat dwarfed by its neighbor, the Gateway Arch.

St. Louis's population grew and expanded westward. By the start of the twentieth century, plans were made for the construction of an artistic masterpiece, a Catholic place of worship unlike anything nearby. The massive granite structure was to be built in sections and covered inside with mosaics and stained-glass windows. Construction of the Cathedral Basilica of Saint Louis took years to complete (ground clearing, 1907; first mass, 1914; consecration, 1926), with artisans brought in from Europe. Locals soon referred to it as the New Cathedral and the original riverfront church as the Old Cathedral.

 **WORSHIP, PLAY, WEAR**

The New Cathedral contains a spectacular display of eighty-three million individual mosaic tiles. The tiles depict scenes from stories in the Bible. "The elaborate mosaics bring a little bit of Europe to St. Louis," says Cathedral Basilica spokesperson Nicole Heerlein. "They are monuments to the test of time, built to the glory of God. We attract tourists, but the buildings are first and foremost a sacred and religious base for St. Louis Catholics."

Fact BOX

St. Louis is unique in that both the Old Cathedral (circa 1830s) and the New Cathedral (early 1900s) have been designated by the pope in Rome as basilicas. Only those Catholic churches with spiritual or historical significance are given this distinction. "It's not all that common to have two basilicas in one city," says Gabe Jones, Archdiocese of St. Louis spokesperson.

NEW CATHOLIC CATHEDRAL. ST. LOUIS. MO.

63217
107

STL is a party city? Welcome to Party Town!

St. Louisans love a good civic party or parade or reason to celebrate.

 **WORSHIP, PLAY, WEAR**

When it comes to parties for say, thousands, St. Louis has it covered. Parties, parades, festivals, and civic celebrations of any kind are enjoyed by St. Louisans of all ages. We're a party town!

St. Louis's celebration of Mardi Gras has become legendary, with two distinct parades. The Grand Parade features floats, krewes, and beads. The Barkus Pet Parade features hundreds of costumed dogs and their owners, plus an occasional pink poodle.

Each March, STL hosts not one but *two* St. Patrick's Day parades. Both claim to be the "official" St. Patrick's Day Parade. It doesn't matter. We love them both. Marching bands, balloons, floats, and thousands of spectators. Even if you're ancestors weren't Irish, it's still a good time.

Other annual celebrations include LouFest Music Festival, Octoberfest and the celebration of all things German, St. Nicholas Greek Festival, the Missouri Botanical Garden's Japanese Festival, and the Fourth of July's Fair St. Louis.

And how did STL become such a festival-loving city? "St. Louis has always been known as a drinking city, what with all the breweries through the years," says *St. Louis Post-Dispatch* columnist Joe Holleman. "But the large-scale celebrations are something relatively new, in the last thirty or so years."

Where the wares were wearable.

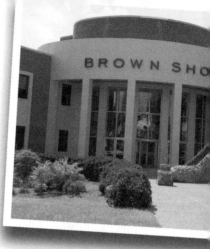

STL's connection to the shoe and clothing industries

St. Louis was for many decades a major hub for shoe and clothing design and production. St. Louis was ideally located in the center of the US, with ready access to railroad and river transportation. That meant raw materials and finished products could enter and leave St. Louis in an efficient manner.

Much of the production and warehouse activity of St. Louis's garment district centered around Washington Avenue. By the 1920s, the garment district encompassed fifteen blocks. Many yesteryear industrial facilities continue to line the busy thoroughfare today but have been repurposed into loft living and office spaces. However, for many years the area was electric with the activity of thousands of workers and the hum of automated machines and delivery vehicles.

Dozens of shoe manufacturers and their headquarters buildings were located in St. Louis, including International Shoe Company; Brown Shoe; Edison Brothers; Friedman-Shelby; Roberts, Johnson & Rand; and Fox-Wohl.

WORSHIP, PLAY, WEAR

Seventy-four garment companies called St. Louis home, including manufacturers of coats, dress shirts, hats, dresses, neckwear, wedding gowns, sleepwear, and lingerie. Innovations born in St. Louis included junior-size clothing and ready-to-wear fashions.

Shannon Meyer is senior curator with the Missouri History Museum. The museum's textile collections include hundreds of clothing items manufactured in St. Louis, some over a hundred years old and in pristine condition. "The History Museum has an amazing collection!" she says.

Fact BOX

Saint Louis Fashion Fund is a two-year-old, nonprofit organization that promotes fashion education in St. Louis and supports emerging designers. In an effort to rekindle interest in the St. Louis fashion industry, the fund recently hired Eric Johnson to coordinate the newly formed Saint Louis Fashion Incubator.

"I am thrilled to return to my hometown for this opportunity to bring the business of fashion back to the city," Johnson says.

"St. Louis was a center of fashion and design, known for its production of hats, gloves, coats, and especially shoes. I look forward to working with the civic and corporate community to make St. Louis a fashion destination once again."

BIBLIOGRAPHY

Books

Auble, John. *A History of St. Louis Gangsters*. St. Louis, MO: National Crime Research Society, 2000.

Barley, Patricia and Joan Woods. *Missouri Life*, Special World's Fair Anniversary Edition, "The Greatest of Expositions." Jefferson City, MO: May-August 1979.

Berger, Henry W. *St. Louis and Empire: 250 Years of Imperial Quest and Urban Crisis*. Carbondale, IL: Southern Illinois University Press, 2015.

Bremer, Jeff. *A Store Almost in Sight*. Iowa City, IA: University of Iowa Press, 2014.

Conard, Howard L. *Encyclopedia of the History of Missouri*, Railroad Articles. St. Louis, MO: Southern History Company, 1901.

Cox, Jeremy R.C. *St. Louis Aviation*. Charleston, SC: Arcadia Publishing, 2011.

Dry, Camille N. *Pictorial St. Louis, the Great Metropolis of the Mississippi Valley: A Topographical Survey Drawn in Perspective, A.D. 1875*. Designed and edited by Richard J. Compton. St. Louis, MO: Knight Publishing, 1979.

Erwin, James W. *The Homefront in Civil War Missouri*. Charleston, SC: The History Press, 2014.

Erwin, Vicki Berger. *Kirkwood*. Charleston, SC: Arcadia Publishing, 2013.

Evans, Mike. *The Blues—A Visual History, 100 Years of Music that Changed the World*. New York, NY: Sterling, 2014.

Faherty, William Barnaby. *The Saint Louis Portrait*. Tulsa, OK: Continental Heritage, Inc., 1978.

Fox, Tim, editor. *Where We Live—A Guide To St. Louis Communities*. St. Louis, MO: Missouri Historical Society Press, 1995.

Gerteis, Louis S. *Civil War St. Louis*. Lawrence, KS: University Press of Kansas, 2001.

Gill, McCune. *The St. Louis Story*. St. Louis, MO: Historical Record Association, 1952.

Hannon, Robert E., editor. *St. Louis: Its Neighborhoods and Neighbors, Landmarks and Milestones*. St. Louis, MO: Buxton & Skinner Printing, 1985.
Harris, Nini. *Downtown St. Louis*. St. Louis, MO: Reedy Press, 2015.

Horgan, James J. *City of Flight*. Gerald, MO: The Patrice Press, 1984.

Hyde, William and Howard L. Conard, editors. *Encyclopedia of the History of St. Louis*, Vol. IV. The Southern History Company, 1899.

Kimbrough, Mary and Margaret W. Dagen. *Victory without Violence*. Columbia, MO: University of Missouri Press, 2000.

Leonard, Mary Delach. *Animals Always—100 Years of the Saint Louis Zoo*. Columbia, MO: University of Missouri Press, 2009.

Lester, Julius. *The Blues Singers: Ten Who Rocked the World*. New York, NY: Hyperion Books for Children, 2001

Magnan, William B. *Streets of St. Louis*. Groton, CT: Right Press, Inc., 1994.

Mormino, Gary Ross. *Immigrants on the Hill: Italian Americans in St. Louis 1882–1982*. Chicago, IL: University of Illinois Press, 1986.

O'Neil, Tim. *Mobs, Mayhem & Murder: Tales from the St. Louis Police Department*. St. Louis, MO: St. Louis Post-Dispatch Books, 2009.

O'Neil, Tim. *The Gateway Arch—An Unlikely Masterpiece*. St. Louis, MO: St. Louis Post-Dispatch Books, 2015.

Pfeiffer, David A. *Bridging the Mississippi: The Railroads and Steamboats Clash at the Rock Island Bridge*. Washington, D.C.: National Archives Prologue Magazine, 2004.

Primm, James Neal. *Lion of the Valley*. St. Louis, MO: Pruett Publishing, 1981.

Sandweiss, Eric. *St. Louis—The Evolution of an American Urban Landscape*. Philadelphia, PA: Temple University Press, 2001.

Santelli, Robert, Holly George-Warren, Holly, Jim Brown, editors. *American Roots Music*. New York, NY: Henry N. Abrams, Incorporated, 2001.

Scharf, Thomas. *History of Saint Louis City and County from the Earliest Periods to the Present Day*. Philadelphia, PA: Louis H. Everts & Co., 1883.

Shepley, Carol Ferring. *Movers and Shakers. Scalawags and Suffragettes. Tales From Bellefontaine Cemetery*. St. Louis, MO: University of Missouri Press, 2008.

Spencer, Thomas M. *The St. Louis Veiled Prophet Celebration—Power on Parade, 1877–1995.* Columbia, MO: University of Missouri Press, 2000.

Stadler, Frances Herd. *St. Louis Day By Day.* St. Louis, MO: The Patrice Press, 1989.

Stepenoff, Bonnie. *The Dead End Kids of St. Louis.* Columbia, MO: University of Missouri Press, 2010.

Stage, Wm. *Fading Signs of St. Louis.* Charleston, SC: The History Press, 2013.

Stage, Wm. *Ghost Signs: Brick Wall Signs in America.* Cincinnati, Ohio: Signs of the Times Publishing Company, 1989.

Stevens, Walter B. *St. Louis: The Fourth City.* Chicago, IL: S.J. Clarke Publishing Company, 1909.

Terry, Elizabeth, John Wright, and Patrick McCarthy. *Ethnic St. Louis.* St. Louis, MO: Reedy Press, 2015.

Toft, Carolyn Hewes. St. Louis: Landmarks and Historic Districts. St. Louis, MO: Landmarks Association of St. Louis, 1988.

Toft, Carolyn Hewes. *The Hill: The Ethnic Heritage of an Urban Neighborhood.* St. Louis, MO: Ethnic Heritage Study Council, 1980.

Winter, William C. *The Civil War in St. Louis—A Guided Tour.* St. Louis, MO: Missouri Historical Society Press, 1994.

Woodcock, Jim. *St. Louis Blues Hockey Club 1967–2002: Note by Note.* St. Louis, MO: Pinnacle Press, 2002.

Newspapers & Other Materials

Advertising Cards (late nineteenth century, early twentieth century), St. Louis, MO. Missouri History Museum printed materials archives.

Batts, Jeannette. "A Sewer Runs Through It," Riverfront Times, Dec. 6, 2000.

Beauchamp, Scott. "The Mystery of St. Louis's Veiled Prophet," The Atlantic, Sept. 2, 2014.

Brown, Lisa. "Schlafly Beer Is 'Recalibrating For Growth,' " St. Louis Post-Dispatch, Jan 16, 2016.

Brown, Lisa. "Urban Chestnut To Open Research Brewery," St. Louis Post-Dispatch, Jan. 12, 2016.

Cassella, William N., Jr. "City-County Separation: The Great Divorce of 1876," *Missouri Historical Society Bulletin*, Jan. 1959.

Christo, Bethany; Shannon Cothran, Liz Miller; and Andrew Mark Veety. "Meat + Carbs = Slingers," *Feast Magazine*, Aug. 28, 2014.

Climate Change and Your Health—St. Louis & Columbia, MO. "Heat in the Heartland." (brochure, date and author unknown).

Collins, Cameron. "The History of the St. Louis Municipal Bath House." nextSTL, Dec. 20, 2012.

Graham, Sara. "6 Best Doughnut Shops In St. Louis," *Riverfront Times*, Jan. 22, 2015.

"Cultural Resource Survey—Old Dutchtown and Benton Park West Survey." Prepared for the City of St. Louis, Missouri, by Historic Preservation Services, LLC. Aug. 30, 3003.

"History of the Saint Louis Zoo Board Book" with unknown author, printed booklet, 2015.

Holleman, Joe. "Spotlight: Last Indian Mound in St. Louis Still Deteriorating," *St. Louis Post-Dispatch*, Oct. 4, 2015.

Holleman, Joe. "Long, Troubled History for Lindbergh Boulevard," *St. Louis Post-Dispatch*, March 5, 2016.

Jarrett, Linda. "Uncover the Tales of Missouri's Cemeteries," *AAA Midwest Traveler*, September/October 2015.

Kehe, Marjorie. "Entrepreneur Joe Edwards Helps make St. Louis Vibrant Again," *Christian Science Monitor*, Dec. 14, 2012.

Krystal, Becky. "Impulsive Traveler: Eagle Watching in Grafton, Ill.," *Washington Post*, Jan. 14, 2011.

"Missouri—The Cave State," Missouri Department of Natural Resources news release with unknown author, March 2014.

Meyerowitz, Robert. "St. Louis's Brick Thieves," *St. Louis Magazine*, June 8, 2011.

Naffziger, Chris. "Old Breweries Tell the Forgotten Legacy of Falstaff Beer In St. Louis," *Riverfront Times*, Feb. 4, 2014.

O'Neil, Tim. "Gilded Age Hucksterism and Phony Census Boost St. Louis," *St. Louis Post-Dispatch*, July 12, 2014.

Perez, A. J. "After Losing Another NFL Team, Unlikely St. Louis Will Be Able to Get Another," *USA Today Sports*, Jan. 14, 2016.

Photographic Images, 1904 Louisiana Purchase Exposition—glass negatives of buildings and displays with various unknown photographers, Missouri History Museum Photograph and Prints Dept.

Pistor, Nick. "Pership or Berlin? A St. Louis Street Name Debate," *St. Louis Post-Dispatch*, Feb. 3, 2014.

Renn, Aaron M. "An Option to the 'Unigov' Example for St. Louis Region." *St. Louis Post-Dispatch*, April 8, 2016.

"Saint Louis Zoo Fact Sheet" with unknown author," 2016.

"Saint Louis Zoo Wildcare Report" with unknown author," printed booklet, 2014.

Sherman, Susan. "Saint Louis Fashion Fund Announces Eric Johnson as Executive Director of the Saint Louis Fashion Incubator." News release from Saint Louis Fashion Fund, Feb. 17, 2016.

Sorkin, Michael. "Lorraine Dieckmeyer Dies: Sold Town's Best Brain Sandwiches." *St. Louis Post-Dispatch*, March 24, 2011.

Staff and Wire Reports. "Cemeteries Aren't Just for the Dead," *St. Louis Post-Dispatch*, Sept. 25, 2015.

Stiles, Nancy. "10 Things You Didn't Know about Ted Drewes Frozen Custard," *Riverfront Times*, June 18, 2014.

Taylor, Betsy. "St. Louis Fights for a Place in Blues History," *USA Today*, Nov. 15, 2009.

"The Shelley House, St. Louis, MO," with unknown author, National Register of Historic Places registration form, April 18, 1988.

Thomas, Scott. "A Pork Steak Primer," *Feast Magazine*, May 31, 2013.

Toler, Lindsay. "13 Words That Have a Different Meaning in St. Louis," *Riverfront Times*, Jan. 28, 2015.

Toler, Lindsay. "Happy 50th Birthday, St. Louis City Flag!" *Riverfront Times*, Feb. 3, 2014.

Wayman, Norbury L. "History of St. Louis Neighborhoods: Downtown." St. Louis Community Development Center, 1978.

Wayman, Norbury L. "History of St. Louis Neighborhoods: Shaw." St. Louis Community Development Center, 1980.

Weiss, Richard. "The Veiled Prophet Returns to St. Louis for Pomp and Scrutiny," *St. Louis Beacon*, July 1, 2011.

Wessels, Gloria. "Put More Bite into Zoo-Museum District's Special Audits," *St. Louis Post-Dispatch*, March 29, 2016.

Websites

"1904 World's Fair—Looking Back at Looking Forward." Retrieved March 3, 2016. http://mohistory.org/FAIR/WF/HTML/Overview/

"A Brief History Of . . . Beer in St. Louis," Retrieved Aug. 31, 2015. http://www.historyhappenshere.org/node/6866

"A Brief History of the Blues." Retrieved May 4, 2016. http://www.allaboutjazz.com/a-brief-history-of-the-blues-by-ed-kopp.php

"About Us—G & W Bavarian Style Sausage Company." Retrieved May 10, 2016. https://www.gwsausage.com/history

"About—Visit the Loop." Retrieved May 6, 2016. http://visittheloop.com/about

"About the ZMD." Retrieved April 7, 2016. http://mzdstl.org/about.html

"Ballparks, Arenas and Stadiums: St. Louis Arena-St. Louis, MO." Retrieved May 9, 2016. http://www.ballparks.phanfare.com/2414471

"Basilica of Saint Louis, King, St. Louis, Missouri (The Old Cathedral)." Retrieved Sept. 4, 2015. http://www.oldcathedralstl.org/history.html

"Beer Guide: Saint Louis, Missouri." Retrieved Aug. 31, 2015. http://www.beeradvocate.com/place/city/32/

"Blueberry Hill—A Landmark St. Louis Restaurant & Music Club." Retrieved May 20, 2016. http://blueberryhill.com/our-story

"Built St. Louis—Vanished Buildings: The Arena." Retrieved May 6, 2016. http://builtstlouis.net/arena01.html

"Built St. Louis: The Watertowers." Retrieved May 6, 2016. http://www.builtstlouis.net/watertowers/watertowers1.html

"Black & White." St. Louis Public Radio. September 4, 2015. www.stlouispublicradio.org/program/black-white

"Blues History—St. Louis Blues History." Retrieved March 9, 2016. http://blues.nhl.com/club/page.htm?id=39464

"Built St. Louis—Dedicated to the Preservation of Historic Architecture in St. Louis, Missouri." Retrieved Sept. 4, 2015. http://www.builtstlous.net

"Catholic Cemeteries of the Archdiocese of St. Louis—Calvary Cemetery." Retrieved Sept. 1, 2015. http://archstl.org/cemeteries/content/view/91/233/

"Charles Lindbergh's Boulevard and the Drive to Rename It," History Happens Here—The Missouri History Museum's blog. March 2, 2010. Retrieved Nov. 9, 2015. http://www.historyhappaneshere.org/archives/1766

"Cherokee Station Business Association—Cherokee Street, St. Louis, Missouri." Retrieved Sept. 4, 2015. http://www.cherokeestation.com/history.html

"City of St. Louis Water Division: Watertowers." Retrieved May 6, 2016. http://www.stlwater.com/watertowers.php

"Climatron Conservatory." Missouri Botanical Garden. Retrieved Sept. 4, 2015. http://www.mobot.org

"Coming in April 2016: Little Black Dress: From Mourning to Night." Missouri History Museum. Retrieved Jan. 15, 2016. http://mohistory.org/node/57334

"Compton Hill Water Tower—City Landmark #13." Retrieved May 6, 2016. https://www.stlouis-mo.gov/government/departments/planning/cultural-resources/city-landmarks/Compton-Hill-Water-Tower.cfm

"Dotage St. Louis: Why Is Everything Brick?" April 14, 2008. Retrieved Sept. 1, 2015. http://stldotage.blogspot.com/2008/04/why-is-everything-brick.html

"Encyclopedia of Missouri History: Railroads." Retrieved Sept. 1, 2015. http://tacnet.missouri.org/history/encycmo/railroads.html

"Explore St. Louis—Cherokee Street." Retrieved Sept. 4, 2015. http://explorestlouis.com/visit-explore/discover/neighborhoods/cherokee-street/

"Explore St. Louis—Civil War History in St. Louis." Retrieved Sept. 1, 2015. http://explorestlouis.com/visit-explore/discover/itineraries/civil-war-history-in-st-louis/

"Foods of Saint Louis, MO." Retrieved Nov. 5, 2015. http://stlplaces.com/stl_foods/

"Freedom's Gateway—St. Louis in the Civil War." Retrieved Sept. 1, 2015. http://www.freedomsgateway.com/CivilWarinStLouis.aspx

"Garage Sales in St. Louis, Missouri." Retrieved Sept. 4, 2015. http://stlouis.bookoo.com/garage-sales-st.-louis-mo.html?r=10.0

"Gateway Arch Completed." Retrieved May 9, 2016. http://www.history.com/this-day-in-history/gateway-arch-completed

"Grant's Farm: Home to History, Wildlife and an Adventure for the Whole Family." Retrieved March 9, 2016. http://www.grantsfarm.com/attractions.html

"History—How This St. Louis Tradition Started." Retrieved Mar. 3, 2016. http://greatforestparkballonrace.com/history

"History—Imo's Pizza." Retrieved Sept. 1, 2015. http://imospizza.com/history/

"History of Barnes-Jewish Hospital." Retrieved May 6, 2016. http://www.barnesjewish.org/About-Us/History

"History of Forest Park." Retrieved March 3, 2016. https://www.stlouis-mo.gov/archive/history-forest-park/early.html

"History of Hodak's, Welcome Home." Retrieved May 10, 2016. http://hodaks.com/history/

"History of St. Louis Children's Hospital." Retrieved May 6, 2016. http://www.stlouischildrens.org/about-us/history

"History of St. Louis Neighborhoods—Marquette-Cherokee." Retrieved Sept. 4, 2015. https://www.stlouis-mo.gov/archive/neighborhood-histories-norbury-wayman/marquette/text17.htm

"History of St. Louis Neighborhoods—The Hill." Retrieved Sept. 1, 2015. https://www.stlouis-mo.gov/archives/neighborhood-histories

"History of the Cathedral Basilica—Cathedral Basilica of St. Louis." Retrieved Sept. 4, 2015. http://cathedralstl.org/parish/parish-history

"Lindbergh Links: One Road, Two Names; the Difference is a City Limit." Retrieved Sept. 4, 2015. http://patch.com/missouri/kirkwood/lindbergh-links-one-road-two-names-the-difference-is5c8d5b33a8

"Look Back 250—Gilded Age Hucksterism and Phony Census Boost St. Louis." Retrieved March 8, 2016. http://www.stltoday.com/news/local/metro/look-back

"Louis H. Sullivan Biography." Retrieved March 23, 2016. www.biography.com/people

"Lou Oldani's Restaurant Claimed to Be the Birthplace of Toasted Ravioli." *St. Louis Post-Dispatch*. Retrieved Aug. 31, 2015. http://www.stltoday.com/news/local/obituaries/

"Missouri Earthquake History." U.S. Geological Survey. Retrieved March 23, 2016. http://www.earthquake.usgs.gov

Missouri History Museum Facebook post. Retrieved Nov. 17, 2015. http://www.facebook.com/search

"Missouri—The Cave State." Missouri Caves Association. Retrieved Apr. 12, 2016. http://missouricaves.com/caves/

"Moonrise Hotel—Joe Edwards." Retrieved May 6, 2016. http://moonrisehotel.com/joe-edwards/

"Mound City on the Mississippi, a St. Louis History." St. Louis Historic Preservation. Retrieved Apr. 19, 2016. http://stlcin.missouri.org/history/structdetail.cfm?Master_ID=2090

"National Blues Museum Strengthens St. Louis' Bond with Genre." Retrieved May 4, 2016. https://www/national_bluesmuseum.org/news/

"Neighborhoods." Retrieved Feb. 15, 2016. http://explorestlouis.com/visit-explore/discover/neighborhoods/

"Old Courthouse." Retrieved May 6, 2016. https://www.nps.gov/jeff/planyourvisit/och.htm

"Open for Business Year-Round!—Ballpark Village." Retrieved Feb. 17, 2016. http://stlouis.cardinals.mlb.com/stl/ballpark/information/index

"Our Beers—Urban Chestnut Brewing Company." Retrieved Jan. 19, 2016. http://urbanchestnut.com/our-beers/

"Physical Growth of the City of Saint Louis." St. Louis City Plan Commission–1969. Retrieved Sept. 4, 2015. https://www.stlouis-mo.gov/archive/ihistory-physical-growth-stlouis/

Pohlmann, Mark. "Stop Sign Warrants," ITE District 4 Journal. Retrieved Apr. 12, 2016. http://www.midwesternite.org/FallJournal/StopSign-Warrants.htm

"Portraits in the Graveyard: An Unexpected Look into the History of Organized Crime in St. Louis." Retrieved March 23, 2016. https://astumblingcontradicition.wordpress.com

"Provelology: The Study of a Made-Up Cheese with a Made-Up Name." Retrieved Dec. 3, 2015. http://www.stltoday.com/lifestyles/food-and-cooking/

"Readers: St. Louis Has Too Many Stop Signs." UrbanReview, Saint Louis. Retrieved Apr. 11, 2016. http://www.urbanreviewstl.com/2014/03/readers-st-louis-has-too-many-stop-signs/

"River des Peres Watershed Coalition." Retrieved Feb. 15, 2016. http:riverdesperes.org/explore/timeline

"Soulard Farmers Market St. Louis." Retrieved Sept. 4, 2015. http://soulardmarketstl.com/about-soulard-market/

"Spirits of St. Louis." Retrieved May 6, 2016. https://enwikipedia.org/wiki/Spirits_of_St._Louis

"St. Louis Beer Guide." Retrieved Aug. 31, 2015. http://stlhops.com/st-lous-beer-guide

"Saint Louis Downtown Map." Saint Louis Front Page. Retrieved April 8, 2016. http://www.slfp.com/CityScapes.html

"St. Louis Cardinals (1960–1987)." Retrieved May 10, 2016. http://wwwsportsencyclopedia.com/nfl/azstl/cardinals.html

"St. Louis City Revised Code Chapter 15.156: Division IX. Miscellaneous Offenses and Regulations: Yard Sales." Retrieved Sept. 4, 2015. http://www.slpl.lib.mo.us/cco/code/data/t15156.htm

"St. Louis Hawks (1955–1968)." http://www.sportsencyclopedia.com/nba/stlhawks.html

"St. Louis, Missouri, Code of Ordinances, ordinance 17.02.500—Stop." Retrieved Apr. 12, 2016.https://www.municode.com/library/mo/st._louis/codes/code_of_ordinances?nodeId=TIT17VETR_DIVITRCO_CH17.02DE_17.02.010GE

"St. Louis Union Station." Retrieved Sept. 1, 2015. http://www.stlouisunionstation.com/about

"St. Patrick's Day Parade." Retrieved Mar. 3, 2016. https://irishparade.org/the-parade/

"Terminal Railroad Association of St. Louis— TRRA History." Retrieved Nov. 9, 2015. http://www.terminalrailroad.com

"The Great Forest Park Balloon Race." Retrieved Mar. 3, 2016. http:stlouis.about.com

"The Great Ice Cream/Frozen Custard Debate," Retrieved Nov. 9, 2015. http://www.chefs.edu/student-life/culinary-central/april-2012/the-great-ice-cream-frozen-custard-debate

"The History of Frozen Custard." Retrieved Sept. 4, 2015. http://www.rebco2000.com/ollies

"The History of IBC Root Beer," Retrieved Feb. 4, 2016. http://www.ibcrootbeer.com/history.aspx

"The History of St. Louis Municipal Bath House," nextSTL, May 6, 2016. https://nextstl.com/2012/12/the-history-of-the-st-louis-municipal-bath-house/

"The Last Standing Mound in Mound St. Louis City Is for Sale." Retrieved Feb. 26, 2016. www.landmarks-stl.org/news

"The Many Mysteries of 'Our' Mostaccioli." St. Louis Post-Dispatch. Retrieved Aug. 31. 2015. https://www.questia.com/newspaper/

"The Mystery of St. Louis's Veiled Prophet." Retrieved Jan. 19, 2016. http://www.theatlantic.com/politics/archive/2014/09

"The Official Site of the St. Louis Cardinals." Retrieved March 23, 2016. http://stlouis.cardinals.mlb.com

"The Rising Fourth City (1890–1904)." St. Louis Turns 250 in 2014. Retrieved Sept. 1, 2015. http://www.stl250.org/crash-course-fourth-city.aspx

"The State & Indian Streets of South St. Louis." Distilled History. Retrieved Apr. 9, 2016. http://www.distilledhistory.com/streets/

"Toasted Ravioli, The Secret of St. Louis." *New York Times*. Retrieved Aug. 31, 2015. http://www.nytimes.com/1987/02/25/

"Twenty-Five Mafia Cities." Retrieved September 1, 2015. http://americanmafia.com

"Twisted History." Retrieved Aug. 31, 2015. http://guspretzels.com

"U.S. Army Corps of Engineers—Eagle Watching." Retrieved Nov. 9, 2015. http://www/mvs.usace.army.mi/missions/recreation/eaglewatching.aspx

"Veiled Prophet Organization—History." Retrieved Jan. 12, 2016. http://www.veiledprophet.org/history

"Visitors Guide to the Middle Mississippi River Valley." Retrieved Nov. 9, 2015. http://www.greatriverroad.com

"Welcome to City Museum, Where Imagination Runs Wild!" Retrieved April 7, 2016. http://www.citymuseum.org/pages/about-us-creative/

Interviews & E-Mails
Anonymous Source, St. Louis Blues Hockey Club: interview with author, March 22, 2016.

Batres, Jose, Hodak's: interview with author, May 17, 2016.

Behle, Pat, Columbia Bottom Conservation Area, Missouri Department of Conversation: interview with author, Feb. 3, 2016.

Bolin, Norma M., lawyer: interview with author, April 1, 2016.

Burkett, Sue, librarian, Kirkwood Historical Society: interview with author, Feb. 26, 2016.

Carlson, Mike, son of co-owner, Schottzie's Bar and Grill: interview with author, Jan. 22, 2016.

Carney, Jon, meteorologist, National Weather Service: e-mail to author, Feb. 18, 2016.

Clanton, Terry, owner, World's Fair Donuts: interview with author, Feb. 26, 2016.

Colligan, Andrew, archivist, Missouri Botanical Garden: interview with author, Feb. 16, 2016.

Cooksey, Talan, Park Avenue Coffee: interview with author, Feb. 16, 2016.

DeWitt, Matt, counselor, Calvary Cemetery: interview with author, Jan. 13, 2016.

Erwin, Jim, writer and Civil War historian: e-mail to author, Feb. 18, 2016.

Gallagher, Susan, director of public relations, Saint Louis Zoo: interview with author, March 9, 2016.

Guinan, Patrick E., University of Missouri Extension state climatologist: e-mail to author, March 16, 2016.

Heerlein, Nicole, spokesperson, Cathedral Basilica of Saint Louis: interview with author, Jan. 19, 2016.

Holleman, Joe, *St. Louis Post-Dispatch*: interview with author, Feb. 16, 2016.

Jones, Gabe, spokesperson, Archdiocese of St. Louis: interviews with author, Jan. 15, 2016, and Jan. 18, 2016.

Kelly, Bill, senior educator, James. S. McDonnell Planetarium at the Saint Louis Science Center: interview with author, Feb. 18, 2016.

Koebbe, Gus III, Gus' Pretzels: interview with author, Jan. 13, 2016.

Kuplent, Florian, brewmeister, Urban Chestnut: interview with author, Jan. 28, 2016.

Lay, Richard, vice president, Bellefontaine Cemetery Association: interview with author, Jan. 13, 2016.

Lowery, Robert Sr., member of St. Louis's Major Case Squad, the St. Louis Strike Force on Organized Crime, and a former Florissant mayor: interview with author, April 6, 2016.

Merkel, Jim, writer: interview with author, Feb. 4, 2016.

Meyer, Shannon, senior curator, Missouri History Museum: interview with author. July 31, 2015.

Rhomberg, Greg R., owner, Antique Warehouse: e-mails to author, Feb. 3, 2016, and Feb. 4, 2016.

Rosen, Rick, Landmarks Association of St. Louis, volunteer coordinator: e-mails to author, Feb. 15, 2016.

Rugg, Marji, owner's daughter, Courtesy Diner/Hampton Ave: interview with author, Jan. 22, 2016.

Runde, Stephen J., director of streets, city of St. Louis: interview with author, Apr. 14, 2016.

Sherman, Susan, for Eric Johnson, Saint Louis Fashion Incubator: interview with author, Feb. 17, 2016.

Spencer, Dr. Thomas M., author and director of honors student affairs, Eastern Illinois University: e-mails with author, Feb. 15, 2016, and March 7, 2016.

Storm, Max, founder, 1904 World's Fair Society, Inc.: interview with author, Jan. 15, 2016.

Torbert, Dr. Benjamin, University of Missouri-St. Louis: e-mails to author, March 9, 2016.

Vogt, Samantha, owner's assistant, Charlie Gitto's: interview with author, Jan. 22, 2016.

Wanninger, Mel, G & W Bavarian Style Sausage Company: interview with author, May 18, 2016.

Weil, Andrew, director, Landmarks Association of St. Louis; e-mails with author Feb. 16, 2016.

Zimmer, Ronald N., American Society of Civil Engineers and Museum of Transportation volunteer: e-mails with author, Feb. 24, 2016.

PHOTO CREDITS

Images not listed below are believed to be in the public domain.

INDEX